A Better Man

One Man's Incredible Journey

Cover design by Gary Asher
Page layout by Jody Conners

ISBN 978-0-945134-43-5

Cover Photo by Christian Heeb
www.heebphoto.com

Other Books
by Rick Steber

Rendezvous
Traces
Union Centennial
Where Rolls the Oregon
Heartwood
Oregon Trail – Last of the Pioneers
Roundup
New York to Nome
Wild Horse Rider
Buckaroo Heart
No End in Sight
Buy the Chief a Cadillac
Legacy
Forty Candles
Secrets of the Bull
Caught in the Crosshairs
A Promise Given
Red White Black
All-Around and the 13th Juror

Tales of the Wild West Series
Oregon Trail
Pacific Coast
Indians
Cowboys
Women of the West
Children's Stories
Loggers
Mountain Men
Miners
Grandpa's Stories
Pioneers
Campfire Stories
Tall Tales
Gunfighters
Grandma's Stories
Western Heroes

www.ricksteber.com

Without your wounds, where would your power be? It is your melancholy that makes your low voice tremble into the hearts of men and women? The very angels themselves cannot persuade the wretched and blundering children of this earth as can one human being who has been broken on the wheels of living. In Love's service, only wounded soldiers can serve.

—Brennan Manning

They hit me, but I'm not hurt!
They beat me, but I don't feel it!
When will I wake up so I can find another drink?

—*Proverbs 23:35*
New International Version Translation

NOTE

I first met Dave Franke during a pick-up basketball game. He was over forty, past his physical prime, but made up for his diminishing athletic talents with aggression: setting bone-jarring screens and charging the lane like a pissed-off rhinoceros. One night, as Dave was driving me home after a game, he abruptly swerved off the highway and pulled into the empty parking lot at the Les Schwab tire store. For a long moment we sat in darkness listening to the engine tick away its heat. And then Dave exhaled a long sigh, almost a groan, and said, "I've got a story you need to hear."

In the telling of that story, Dave revealed a facet of his diverse and challenging personality that he seldom allowed anyone to view. It was a story rich, powerful and laced with raw emotions. Dave seemed almost buoyant, as though he was momentarily releasing himself from the oppressive weight of self-expectations, guilt, regret and grief. He spoke with such deep passion that several times he broke down; his voice quivered and quaked and he sobbed unashamedly as he struggled to reveal a story so compelling it stayed with me for three long decades. Now the time has finally come to relate this true narrative—to tell of Dave's desperate search to find the better man.

Chapter One

Make no bones about it, Dave Franke is a man's man; tall, as ruggedly built as a safe, and equally competent as a cowboy, carpenter, contractor, bridge builder and business tycoon. Although he started with nothing, he is a self-made millionaire many times over. But place Dave around people in a social setting and there is something in all his confidence and power that makes women curious and men feel threatened. Invariably he comes across to others as standoffish, as though he views himself as hand-picked and placed on this earth to be the herd bull, perfectly capable of driving away any potential rival. Scratch that thin veneer of ego and find a spiritual man, complex, flawed with personal demons and chock-full of confusing contradictions.

*****

"I WILL HAVE YOU AT FORTY"

Those words, delivered soft and lyrical and yet forceful and compelling, rolled like a wild thunderstorm over the countryside of Powell Butte. During the mid-1970s this ranching and farming community in rural Central Oregon was transitioning itself to become an upscale recreational development. Dirt-poor homesteaders had worked themselves into early graves; and widows dumped the cows at auction, called a real estate broker and high-tailed it for Palm Beach, San Diego or Boca Rotan. In other instances, the sons and daughters of the original homesteaders sold the land so rich in family history to get-rich-quick developers who quickly carved out subdivisions of cute five- and ten-acre parcels.

Grandiose mansions were built so views of Houston Lake and the chain of snowcapped peaks in the Cascade Mountain Range were artfully centered in picture windows; windows which migrating birds never saw, and the twisted bodies of colorful birds with broken necks collected beneath the windows like dead soldiers littering a battlefield. The newcomers brought with them their metropolitan self-indulgent attitudes and loudly complained to the county sheriff about their neighbors— the slow tractors on the roads, the foul smell of feedlots, the bawling calves at weaning time and the *chunk-chunk-chunk* of bailers operating at night when the dew was on the hay.

"I WILL HAVE YOU AT FORTY"

The Franke family had bought a ranch and built an extravagant home overlooking Houston Lake, but they were an anomaly. Dave and his wife, Peggy, having grown up farther east in real ranching country, had moved to Powell Butte so their four daughters would at least get a taste of rural living. Each of the girls had her own horse, was expected to show a steer at the 4-H fair, participate in maintaining the family herd of registered Simmental cattle, and perform a host of chores in the morning before catching the yellow bus that took them to school.

Now Dave sat alone, drinking Black Velvet from an expensive highball glass, the whiskey straight, not diluted with mixer, water, not even chunks of ice floated on the surface. Straight. Maybe the whiskey would dull some of Dave's pain, but it sure as hell was never going to solve the host of financial problems crushing him, grinding him down into a bottomless pit of depression and despair.

"I WILL HAVE YOU AT FORTY"

The sun skidded and skipped from one cloud to the next until it fell behind the distant mountains. The sky caught fire—reds and yellows mostly, but also a threatening blue-black at the fringes that grew in size and slowly supplanted the lively sunset colors. This was the evening Dave was turning forty years old and it should have been a happy occasion. It was not.

Did the voice—*I WILL HAVE YOU AT FORTY*—that echoed over the landscape, scare Dave? Hell yes it terrified him, and caused him to doubt his sanity. The first time he heard the dire warning he had been taking a gulp of whiskey and was so shocked he stopped and looked anxiously around, searching but failing to find the source. He glanced in the direction of the cattle and horses, hoping to detect a sign of alarm from them, but they were oblivious to all but the sweet taste of green pasture grasses. Yet there was no denying what he had heard; the strange timbre of the soft but firm voice, the cadence of each word, the ominous message—*I WILL HAVE YOU AT FORTY*.

Dave grasped that the voice could not be of this earth—this dimension—it had to emanate from somewhere beyond any normal convention. That truth seemed absurd, even crazier than if he had actually been hearing voices, and for a fleeting moment Dave tried to deny what he knew in his heart with absolute certainty. The voice was God. And God was saying He was going to have Dave at forty. What the hell did that even mean? Was Dave about to die? Or was he going to become the latest convert in the growing movement of born again Christians? What did God want from him? Why was He wasting His time on a sinner like Dave? Dave felt completely unworthy of God's attention, His effort.

"Bullshit," muttered Dave, and then addressing God, or whoever, or whatever, was the source of that forewarning, he grumbled, "Why don't you just leave me the hell alone?"

All Dave wanted was to sit where he was sitting—with that million dollar view of lake and snowcapped mountains—under the spreading branches of what he had come to call his *drunk tree*, drowning his sorrows with alcohol and wallowing in his monetary woes. Most of those troubles were caused by a nationwide recession brought on by restrictive governmental policies and alarmingly high interest rates which had all but destroyed the building boom. Dave had ridden that boom to the very pinnacle of economic success, becoming rich beyond any expectations he could have had growing up on the cattle and sheep ranch out of Dayville. Now he felt trapped in a downward spiral and was in the process of losing everything he had worked so hard to attain.

At the height of his glory, Dave had purchased and subdivided huge chunks of property in a circle surrounding what was fast becoming the resort community of Bend, Oregon; an area inhabited mostly by California refugees, a Birkenstock and veggie burger crowd escaping the rat race of their own making, selling their homes and moving north with cash-laden pockets. Dave fueled his home and commercial construction business—the largest in the state of Oregon—with a million-dollar-a-month payroll. He built the house at Powell Butte and had taken on the giant responsibility of purchasing the Franke home ranch—the Tri-Creek Ranch near Dayville, 11,000 deeded acres and a government grazing allotment to an additional 44,000 acres—from his father and uncle. But now the building of homes and commercial developments had come to a jolting standstill. Banks called in their loans and most of Dave's business holdings were gone. The home ranch was sold for pennies on the dollar. Projects went into default. Millions of dollars just vanished. And then that damn voice and the alarming threat. Dave lifted his glass once more and allowed the fiery brown liquid to slide down his throat.

I WILL HAVE YOU AT FORTY.

Chapter Two

Dave could not rid himself of that haunting voice—*I will have you at forty*. It drove him headlong toward a crucial crossroad in his life; a point where he would be forced to make a choice. If he continued on the road he was traveling—falling headlong into the abyss of financial loss and medicating himself with booze—it would most certainly lead to even more pain, heartache and his eventual self-destruction. But if Dave veered away and chose another path he would likely have to follow an ambiguous trail filled with risky twists and turns, chuckholes of indecisiveness and improbability. Each step of the way was fraught with hidden dangers. And what awaited him at the end of that journey? The destination was unknown. His final choice might very well be to simply give in and follow his father's footsteps, to trust in the Lord as his savior and pursue the road to salvation. Dave had never been willing to accept that choice. He loved and respected his father, but no, the godly way was not a path Dave could accept. Not yet he could not.

*****

By the mid 1970s, Dave Franke had the reputation of being an entrepreneurial tycoon. He had millions of dollars in the bank and nearly unlimited credit at his disposal. He was the golden boy of the Bend building community and controlled nearly every major development that was going on in Central Oregon. In addition, he was blessed with a beautiful wife— Peggy Melton, his childhood sweetheart—four daughters, a dream home on 300 acres, and he was in the process of buying the Franke home ranch from his father, Milo, and uncle, Clarence.

But during the years of the Jimmy Carter presidency the national economy turned upside down. Dave was forced to siphon capital from his construction company to finance the ranch. When interest rates went through the roof—rising to 24 percent—home and commercial development came to a screeching halt. No one in his right mind was willing to pay such exorbitant interest rates. When the crash hit, Dave was forced to liquidate property at substantial losses. For a time he was able to keep his construction company solvent by consolidating debt as the banks and lending institutions fell like dominoes.

As the recession tightened its death grip, some of the smaller Bend construction companies simply packed up their tools and slipped out of town. Dave was under the mistaken belief that his company was insulated and could ride out what he perceived to be a short downturn in the economy. He was armed with a glut of approved subdivisions, owned over 100 rental units and had warehouses tied up with long-term leases. His company office was staffed with six employees, and a sales team operated Stagecoach Realty, his real estate division.

*****

The herd of registered Simmental cattle grazing on pasture at the Powell Butte ranch was collateral for a $40,000 chattel mortgage held by Farm Credit in the nearby community of Redmond, Oregon. The loan was coming due. Dave met this challenge head-on. He marched into the credit union, strolled past the line of female tellers confined in caged cubicles, and went directly to the manager's office where he plopped down in an expensive leather chair. Dave, dressed in his normal attire—long sleeve western shirt with pearl snaps, blue jeans, cowboy hat and boots—was a contrast to the pudgy middle-aged manager wearing banker gray, his suit coat a summer weight weave, blue silk tie, gold stick pin and matching gold cufflinks. The manager looked up and over the top of a pile of loose papers scattered across his desk, and frowned. Every construction company in Central Oregon was facing financial ruin and seeing Dave Franke, the owner of the largest construction company in the state, sitting across from him, was not a sight that pleased the manager, and yet he possessed the professionalism to replace the frown with a semblance of a smile.

The manager hesitated for a moment and then asked, "What can I do for you?"

Dave bluntly stated that Farm Credit held a note on his herd of cattle that was coming due, and he was probably going to have to let the credit union have the cattle because he did not have the money to cover the note. With that said, Dave removed his cowboy hat and dragged a shirtsleeve across his brow to add emphasis to the dire hopelessness of his predicament. He replaced the hat and allowed the manager to stew in silence. It was obvious the manager was in the banking business, not the ranching business and sure as hell did not want a herd of cattle on his hands. He would have to find adequate pasture for the cattle, and locate a willing buyer. Money was tight. The buyers who had a few extra bucks in their pockets were tight fisted. Chances were, if Farm Credit took the cattle, its investment would never be recouped. This realization troubled the manager a great deal. He did not want cattle. He wanted money.

"Tell you what," said Dave. "If you're willing to work with me, I'll see what I can do; pay so much on the dollar."

The manager, taking renewed interest in the conversation, wanted to know, "How much?"

"Don't know, depends," drawled Dave. "I'll round up what I can, bring it in; you make the final decision if it's enough."

A few days later Dave returned to the manager's office. He dragged a wad of bills from his shirt pocket—hundred dollar bills—and fanned the money across a corner of the manager's desk. He owed $40,000 on the cattle, but even at a glance it was clearly evident there was not that amount laid out on the desk.

The manager's eyes widened slightly. "How much?" he wanted to know.

Dave ignored the question, said, "What I want is for you to release my 4-F brand and give me clear title to my cattle." He paused to let that sink in and then finished by saying, "All I could get; 20 grand." He pushed the money a few inches closer toward the manager.

The manager raised his hands in mock exasperation and announced, "In all my years of banking I've never agreed to take 50 cents on the dollar. I can't do it."

Dave reached to scoop up the bills, but his hands hesitated a moment as he asked, "When do you want to pick up the cattle?"

The manager pushed back his chair with a sudden rush, stood and announced, "I'll be right back." He left the room like a whirlwind sweeping across a flat. Dave waited, and he waited some more. He played with the money, picking up the bills and fanning them like playing cards in his hands. The manager returned. He deliberately shut the door behind him. He paced fretfully between the door and his desk, looking down, refusing to look up at Dave who continued to silently sit and hold the money in plain sight.

"Goddammit!" groused the manager as he flopped onto his chair. "Why are you doing this to me?"

Dave, his voice laced with genuine sincerity, replied, "I'm doing the best I can."

Once again the manager got to his feet and left the room, returning after a few anxious minutes with two pieces of paper he thrust in Dave's direction. Dave took the release for the 4-F brand, and the release of the chattel mortgage to his cattle. He handed over the cash.

Later that evening, as Dave was explaining to Peggy what had transpired, she wanted to know how Dave knew the manager would take the deal.

"Greed," said Dave with a grin. "He couldn't stand to walk away from the money I was offering because he wasn't sure he could get more. I was saving him a headache; simple as that."

Even though one pressure had been alleviated, Dave still felt the overwhelming weight of all he had worked to accumulate falling around him like an avalanche, suffocating him under the weight of it all. He turned, as he always did, to alcohol. But as he drank the voice returned—*I will have you at forty*. Dave's day of reckoning was fast approaching, the day when he would be forced to choose which path he would follow.

*****

Dave's father, Milo Franke, was born in Iowa and raised on the family farm. At the age of 13, while working a team of horses in a field pulling a two-bottom plow, Milo had a spiritual awakening. God spoke, telling Milo he had been chosen and was to spend his life spreading the word of the gospel. The boy never questioned that encounter and obediently accepted a life devoted to God. During Milo's lifetime—all 75 years—his faith remained strong and unwavering. He never smoked, or drank alcohol, never spoke the Lord's name in vain and was a faithful family man, a godly man who lived his religion.

During the years of the Dust Bowl and the Great Depression, the Franke family lost their farm in Iowa for $1,200 in unpaid taxes. They came west and settled in Portland, Oregon. Milo completed the eighth grade and promptly quit school. He was big for his age, unusually strong, and worked for a time milking cows on a dairy in the Willamette Valley before taking a job as a logger in the woods of the Coast Range. He bucked logs for $75 a month, plus room and board. Although Milo had never studied to become a minister, he read the Bible every morning and evening and on Sundays began preaching to the loggers.

A family of itinerant farm workers on their way to the Willamette Valley to pick hops attended one of Milo's services. Milo fell in love with one of the girls, Pearl Biggs, and after a brief courtship they were married on April 16, 1935. Milo was 18 years old and Pearl was 16 years old. A daughter, Loretta Mae, was born to the Franke family in 1938.

In early 1940, Pearl suffered a tubal pregnancy, was hospitalized and died suddenly. Pearl had been the love of Milo's life and the loss caused him to be paralyzed with grief. He could not care for his daughter and could not even rise from his bed until one day a vision of Pearl appeared in Milo's room. She stood beside his bed in a wispy, white gown. The image leaned over and kissed Milo on the forehead, kissed him seven times. Milo felt the softness of each kiss. He felt the muscles in her lips tremble ever so slightly. He counted each of the seven kisses and knew from the teachings of the Bible that the number seven denotes a godlike perfection. He reached for Pearl, but like a curl of fog, she vanished. With her disappearance, Milo was momentarily heartbroken, and yet the apparition had a long-lasting positive effect on Milo, inspiring him to rise from his bed and call for his daughter. The following day he returned to work in the woods.

Only a few short months after becoming a widower, Milo met 20-year-old Evelyn Schroeder at a church social and quickly married her on July 6, 1940. Evelyn was the oldest of seven children born to Ernest and Katherine (Friesen) Schroeder. Upon marrying Milo, Evelyn became the mother to Loretta, and during their 52 years of marriage, Milo and Evelyn would add four more children to the family, three boys and a girl.

For a short time the Franke family lived near the coastal town of Siletz. They soon moved to Eastern Oregon, where Milo went to work on the John Hudspeth logging crew. The family lived in the town of Mitchell, in an apartment behind a saloon. When Milo was not working in the woods, he devoted his time and energy to building a church. When the structure was completed, Milo continued to work in the woods as well as becoming the pastor of the Mitchell Assembly of God Church. Evelyn, who was also a devout Christian, taught Sunday school and led Bible studies.

It was while they were living in Mitchell that their oldest son, Don, was born, followed by twin boys, Dave and Dan, born July 29, 1945. Doctor Wood, from Prineville, delivered the twins and informed Milo his normal delivery fee was $25 per child, but since he was a new doctor and had never delivered twins, there would be no charge for the delivery.

Milo was busy working and preaching. The raising of the children fell mostly to Evelyn. When it came to young children, Evelyn's theory was that every problem could be cured by a cookie or a piece of pie. She also followed a strict interpretation of the covenants as set forth in the Bible and was not one to spare the rod and spoil the child.

*****

It had been Milo who preached the folksy principal—*If you have to eat crow best get with it because the longer you wait the harder it is to swallow*—and eventually Dave woke up to the fact his construction company could not be saved. The day came when he walked into his business complex, terminated his entire staff, closed the real estate division and locked the doors to Franke Construction Company on his way out. He concentrated on trying to get what he could from the multitude of contracts he was carrying on the books.

Dave made a deal with a group of realtors from Portland who had purchased 15 duplexes. They owed $85,000 on a note. Dave offered to mark down the loan if they paid $65,000 cash. They paid.

An insurance executive, who had gone out on a limb speculating on Bend properties, owed Dave $80,000. Dave called him and offered, "I'll be at the title company at 3 p.m. today. Here is what I want you to do; put $40,000 in cash in an envelope and lay it on the seat of my pickup. I'll be watching, and as soon as you open the door and put the envelope on the seat, I'll sign off on your loan and give you a clear deed." The deal was done. Dave got his cash.

During this difficult time, at every turn, Dave was kept busy trying to pull yet another proverbial rabbit out of the hat. He was powerless to forestall the collapse of his construction empire and was kept busy gathering as much cash money as he could, as quickly as he could, and consequences be damned. He had no recourse but to walk away from jobs that were not yet completed, sometimes collecting his machinery in the dark of night, and yet his personal pride, and a strict sense of right and wrong, propelled him to make sure his subcontractors were paid in full. He did not want working men to suffer. It was the lending institutions and bonding companies that had been all too willing to advance loans during the high flying days of the building boom that were forced to suffer the brunt of the financial losses. They lost untold millions of dollars.

Dave paid a humbling and heavy price for his wheeling and dealing. To dull the pain of his humiliation, and ease his conscience—and to give himself energy and courage—he drank. He drank at least a fifth of Black Velvet a day, oftentimes more. When the charade played out and he was dead broke, Dave came to that crossroad in his life and was forced to make a hard decision. In making that decision, and for years after, he would consider himself a spineless coward who gave in to his demon and abandoned his family.

*****

A friend told Dave that the construction business was still going strong in Apple Valley, California, a distant suburb of Los Angeles, located at the southern tip of the Mojave Desert; a dry, ugly place with fierce winds that blew constantly. Dave decided to go there. By choosing to follow that road, Dave would be leaving his wife and family in Central Oregon. They would have to fend for themselves. Dave justified his decision by guessing his daughters—teenagers and younger—were unaware of his dire financial situation and their lives would go on without much interruption; except they would no longer have to deal with their alcoholic father who was angry most of the time and quick with outbursts of cussing. In his absence, it would be up to Peggy to stand tall for the family, answer the hounding of the many creditors, and follow through on the bankruptcy of Franke Construction, Inc. Dave convinced himself that he was leaving his family and troubles behind and driving to Apple Valley to rebuild his construction business. He was starting over. But in his most lucid moments, when he was between drinks, he knew he was simply escaping and going somewhere he could drink and be accountable to absolutely nobody. Alcohol was in control. It was alcohol that was making him unreasonable, irate, embittered and desperate.

Dave had always considered himself to be the man in charge and the backbone of the family. From his humble beginnings as a preacher's son, with guts and guile, he had built the largest construction company in Oregon. Now his company was all but gone and Dave was bailing out for California. There was a good chance he might never come home, and if he did, he might not have a family to come home to. He was risking it all and for what; another drink, and another after that? What did it matter? God had spoken—*I will have you at forty*—and Dave was living each moment of each day in constant fear of that prophecy, that threat, coming true.

*****

Dave talked to Peggy—not about the voice that he kept hearing over and over again; he told no one about that voice—but he did share his plan to leave her and the family in the big house overlooking Houston Lake while he moved to Southern California to seek work. She cried and asked if there was some other possibility; could the family move to California with him? Dave shook his head. He explained that a lot of families were sacrificing during the recession; said he had to go where he could find work. He promised to send money home. They talked for a long time. Dave steadfastly maintained he was going to the desert to rebuild his construction company. He skillfully avoided the ugly truth, that alcohol was now making the decisions, and that the family be damned.

Then Dave shocked Peggy by producing a thick handful of hundred dollar bills. He spread them across the pool table, and when he was done he turned to Peggy and announced. "Two hundred thousand—that should carry you and the girls for a while." He further augmented that display of currency with the announcement, "In the top desk drawer is a million dollar term life insurance policy, paid for the next five years. You are named as the sole beneficiary. If I don't make it back, cash it."

By the time Dave had spoken those words he was crying; tears of pain, or relief, or a mixture of both were running freely down his ruddy cheeks. Peggy had never seen Dave cry like this, and his tears frightened her. She stood rooted to the spot, looking at the money on the pool table while Dave left the room and poured himself another drink. Peggy was filled with a strange sense of foreboding; a combination of fear and elation. Without Dave she was afraid of what the future might bring, but on the other hand, she was relieved she and her girls would no longer be forced to live with Dave's drinking, his sullenness, despair, anger and moodiness. And then she experienced a tremendous wave of guilt for even acknowledging her feelings of liberation from the domination of her alcoholic husband.

Dave never went to bed. At some point during the night he simply departed from the family's home at Powell Butte, driving his three-year-old GMC three-quarter-ton pickup truck and towing his 22-foot Terry Trailer. As he turned onto Houston Lake Road he never looked back to reflect on whether he would see his wife and daughters again. He was too busy working the cap off a whiskey bottle. He drank freely. The whiskey had the expected kick, but it seemed cushioned, like whiskey wrapped in soft cotton, and by the time he reached La Pine—the town south of Bend straddling Highway 97—he was so drunk he opened the door to vomit and kept driving. He drove and drank all the way to Apple Valley where he alone would have to face the devastating reality of his alcoholism. Most likely he would drink himself to death, and die out there on the broad sweep of the desert landscape. He viewed his situation as hopeless, and almost welcomed his defeat.

I will have you at forty.

Chapter Three

After building the church in Mitchell, Oregon, Milo moved the family, in 1946, to the nearby community of Dayville, where he became the pastor at the Valley Chapel Church. It was the perfect church, small and intimate—painted a sinless white—a gathering spot for the community. When his congregation became too large for the Valley Chapel Church, Milo began building a bigger church, laying the pumice blocks himself, while his family lived in a log home adjacent to the new church.

Milo had a very strong commitment to God, but preaching alone would not support the Franke family. Milo could do most anything and he hired out to log, ranch and help with farming. During his tenure in Dayville, Milo served as the minister at the funerals of at least 600 parishioners, friends and acquaintances. He dug each grave by hand, often bringing his sons along to help with the digging. As a preacher, Milo also married about as many people as he buried. He was well-respected and well-loved in the community he served.

Milo was a charitable man, and when Evelyn's mother died at age 56 from breast cancer, he welcomed her youngest son, Jim Schroeder, born in 1941, into his family and raised him like a fourth son. Milo finished building his second church in Dayville and that same year, 1954, he acquired a large property, the old McDonald Ranch. The McDonalds had lost a son in a car wreck, and without anyone to take over the ranch, they decided to sell. The McDonalds carried the contract for $88,000 and Milo, with his partner and brother, Clarence, took possession of 11,000 acres of deeded land, a 44,000-acre summer-grazing allotment in the Blue Mountains, two John Deere tractors and 250 head of cattle. Milo moved his family to the ranch, and when his duties as the pastor were required, Milo made the 10-mile trip to town.

For nine-year-old Dave, the ranch quickly became his life and his passion. He loved being alone, working horses and cattle and riding through the hills. Dave was big for his age and a quick learner; shoeing horses, breaking horses, doctoring livestock, moving cattle, putting up hay and becoming proficient with a lariat. He broke his first horse before he was 10, learning the techniques of how to gentle and train a green horse from a neighbor and seasoned horse trainer, Joe Martin. By the time Dave was a teenager, folks from around the area were hiring him for day work at brandings, turnouts and gatherings, as well as bringing in horses for him to break and train.

Dave started a horse—most were four-year-olds that had never been ridden or even haltered—by corralling the horse, roping its front feet and putting the horse on the ground. With the horse incapacitated, Dave was able to begin the gentling process. The horse soon learned it was a matter of trusting the young cowboy and usually, within a relatively short period of time, the horse submitted to a halter. Dave taught the green horses to lead by using a whip to tap one leg and then the other, while he gently applied pressure on the lead rope, all while encouraging the horse with words of kindness and respect. Once the horse was leading, Dave tied up a hind leg so the animal could not kick, strike, or move away. He then introduced the blanket, the saddle and finally the bridle and bit. As the horse began giving to the bit, and turning his head, Dave tied the reins to the cinch ring and released the leg that had been tied. The horse was forced to give to the bit as it moved around the corral. After that the reins were switched to the opposite side and the horse was driven the other way. Next came a session with long reins, with Dave driving the horse in circles; to the left and then to the right like a workhorse would be driven. The mount was now ready to be ridden and Dave made sure the animal was comfortable with weight on its back by stepping up and putting a foot in the stirrup, lying across the saddle, and finally when the horse was used to having weight on his back, Dave swung up and onto the saddle.

Dave normally charged a hundred bucks for breaking a horse—big money in those days—but some ranchers preferred to give a horse in exchange for each horse that was broke to ride. That arrangement allowed Dave to double his income because there was always a ready market for a well-broke horse.

*****

Milo purchased a band of sheep—including rams and 1,500 ewes—from Black Hanson, a rancher from Long Creek. Herder, Mike Corley, came with the deal. His pay was $200 a month and room and board. His room was most often nothing more than a tent pitched in a clearing in the forest, and his board was what could be brought to him on packhorses. Once a year, Mike took a week off to visit his family in Long Creek. Otherwise he dedicated himself to staying with the sheep.

Milo wintered his band on the Franke ranch, and after lambing season, the sheep were trailed overland 100 miles to the forest allotment on Greenhorn Mountain. The drive took a couple weeks. The route meandered along the John Day River to Kimberly, Monument, Long Creek, Bear Creek, over Dixie Summit at Austin, down to the town of Bates and due north above Howard Meadows. The sheep were kept on this forest allotment until the weather turned cold and then the drive was reversed. Dave and his brothers helped on the sheep drives, and it was Dave who usually volunteered to lead a pair of pack horses to resupply Mike every couple weeks during the warm weather months. Oftentimes Dave found excuses to stay over at sheep camp where he enjoyed the hunting, fishing and solitude of the mountains.

*****

Within a few weeks of setting up his trailer in the Mojave Desert, Dave had lined up several small construction projects, as well as locating an investor and was breaking ground on a large warehouse with office space. From sunrise to sunset he worked hard in the oppressive desert heat. There was no rain. It never rained, and it never rained, and it never rained some more. It never rained so much as a solitary drop. It refused to rain. It did not rain in the day, and it sure as hell did not rain at night. Dave studied the sky as he had done in Oregon, and there was never any hint of rain on the horizon. The closest the inexhaustible jet blue sky ever came to producing moisture was the sudden appearance late one afternoon of three small puffs of clouds above the bald-faced mountains. These clouds lurked long enough to cast decisive shadows, as dark as purple ponds, but the respite was short-lived. The clouds disappeared and once again the landscape was smacked solid with the brutal heat of the desert.

Dave suffered, worked and drank. His only concession to his work was that during the day he switched from whiskey to vodka because the smell of vodka was less noticeable. On occasions, he frequented the local bars where he was restored by drink and the sleazy gloom of the bars' masculine interiors; the all too common rumble of voices, music and drinking. He filled his nostrils with the odors of stale beer, cigarette smoke and the slightly rancid fat of french fries and hamburgers cooked on a grill. If the barmaid was pretty, Dave might waste a little time flirting with her, and when he departed he left behind a sizable tip, lingering a moment at the door, waiting for her to flash him a teasing smile and tuck away the money.

When he was not working, Dave preferred to hunker down in the seclusion and safety of his trailer. He drank alone and he drank hard and with a mean vengeance. He remained angry; angry at governmental policies that led to his business failings in Oregon, angry at the financial institutions that had called his loans, angry at those he had trusted and done business with, those who had not met the obligations they had agreed to during the heyday of the Central Oregon building boom. But Dave saved his bitterest anger and directed it at himself and his personal shortcomings.

Most evenings the predictable desert sun streaked and stained the western skyline with colors as bright as a salmon fillet, turning to a corrupted pinkish-orange and fading to darkness. Quiet rushed in and settled like a thick wool blanket tucked over the land and the moon rose and bathed the entire broad valley in its white light while the evening star appeared, hanging low in the sullen sky. Swirling bats and swooping nighthawks were kept busy working for whirring bugs, and every once in a while an old chunk of iron that had been noodling around in space for a couple billion years came tumbling down hot and fast—traveling at eight miles a second—igniting as a shooting star and leaving, for a few fleeting seconds, the imprint of its arc on the human retina.

It was in those gloomy moments of night that Dave missed Peggy and his family the most. It made his loneliness—his exile to the desert—even more difficult for him to endure. At night Dave drank and brooded. He tried to sleep but tossed and turned in his sleeping bag on the couch, eyes open, watching shadows flit and scurry across the ceiling of the trailer like lost tumbleweeds rolling in slow motion across the desert floor. Sometimes, when he dozed off, he dreamed of riding in the hills, working cattle, enjoying nature around him and breathing in the sweet air and solitude of the sprawling home ranch where he was raised; other times he yearned to be with Peggy and his girls—to once again be a part of his family—so much so that he awoke with tears flooding his eyes. Isolation consumed him. He feared night almost as much as he feared his drinking. But there was nothing he could do about night, and there was nothing he could do about his drinking. His instincts, basic and primal, remained the same; to be aggressive, to dominate and control the world around him, and it was his demon that forced him to drink.

Outside, on the open landscape, the coyotes were busy calling down the moon as Dave drank himself into a stupor of rage and shame; stranded by receding sleep, his mind flopping in the wide margins of his consciousness like a worthless carp tossed on the riverbank. Responsiveness turned and twisted, tried to dive, floundered against the immovable, thrashed in panic and pain, and he came awake. He laid staring at the ceiling of the cheaply built Terry Trailer, just as he had been doing when he last remembered; mouth as dry as hot sand, eyeballs burning, head pulsating with a dull throb. His stomach was as bad as a sick dog. He wanted to vomit. He was frowning in his agony and pinching his brows down tight against the light. His kidneys hurt and he needed to take a piss, but was afraid if he did he would piss blood. All was silent. Soon the rising sun dragged into existence yet another red-hot poker day. The breath in Dave's throat suddenly sounded franticly loud. Damn, he needed a drink and reached blindly, wincing, scrabbling fingers fumbling, groping for the neck of his lover, finding her and bringing her toward his thirsty lips. Again that contemptible voice threatened him—*I will have you at forty*— and he could not wait for his next birthday to roll around. He drank to kill the voice. He drank to kill time. He drank to kill his suffering, and he drank to kill his loneliness.

*****

While Milo remained busy earning a living for his family, ranching and ministering, the raising of the Franke children fell mostly to Evelyn. She helped with their homework, dispensed hugs when needed, cared for the sick and meted out punishment for any grievous misdeeds. For the most part the Franke children were well-behaved, like a preacher's kids should be, but Dave was the problem child. When he swore or talked back, his mother washed his mouth out with Ivory soap. When he failed to complete his homework he was forced, after chores, to sit at the kitchen table, under the watchful eye of his mother, and finish the assignments. Major infractions caused Evelyn to bring out the leather whip she kept in a drawer in her bedroom. She became so proficient at wielding that whip, she could double-stroke Dave, spanking him twice, before his feet returned to the ground.

There was a wildness in Dave that could not be explained. None of the other Franke kids had that rowdiness in their personalities. Dave's growing up years seemed to be ruled by temptations, and he allowed very few temptations to pass him by. He was big and broad shouldered, never shy, loved to laugh and was a tease to the point of being irritating. He specialized in outrageous yarns, walked with an athletically loose yet purposeful stride, and when he got behind the wheel he drove fast and recklessly. He drank alcohol at an early age and loved to chase girls. He lacked any semblance of respect for authority; nobody could tell Dave Franke what to do. He had self-confidence and was at ease in stores and cafés and around adults as well as kids his own age. His first gun was a family owned Winchester single shot .22, a great gun to learn to make shots count. He killed cans, soda bottles, road signs, telephone insulators and then rabbits and other game. The first gun he bought with his own money was a 12 gauge Long Tom shotgun. He became proficient at shooting quail and chukar on the wing.

When Dave was 11 years old he went hunting with his Grandpa Schroeder—an old man with failing eyesight—and he told Dave to use his rifle, and promised if Dave killed a buck, he could have the rifle. Dave shot a trophy four-point buck and Grandpa Schroeder, true to his word, gave Dave his rifle. Dave was 13 when he killed his first elk, a cow on Greenhorn Mountain that was used for camp meat at the sheep camp.

Dave became skillful at dressing game. His speed and efficiency would have been the envy of most butchers.

Only a few of Dave's traits were admirable. He had a hair-trigger temper and a tendency when he got mad to take the Lord's name in vain. He got into fistfights—he was big and strong for his age and usually won, even against older kids—was defiant to teachers and searched for cigarette butts and smoked them until they burned his lips. Anything contrary or ornery, Dave Franke was all for giving it a try. It was as though he went out of his way to disprove the fact he was the *preacher's son.*

Dave's rebellious ways were even more glaring in light of his twin brother. The two of them seemed to invite comparison even though their only similarity was that they both belonged to the same family tree. In almost every way, Dan was the perfect angel; well-mannered, respectful, courteous and polite. He was tall and slender with a determined set to his shoulders. He had a pleasant look about him and could even be considered handsome. His appearance was that of a sincere young man who could be trusted. At a very early age—he was barely a teenager—Dan announced he had experienced a calling, and planned to follow in his father's footsteps and become a preacher.

Despite Dave's defiant ways, the only instance of Milo ever actually reprimanding his son for his unruly behavior was the time Dave was breaking a bay stud and Milo came to the corral to watch. Maybe Dave subconsciously was aware of his father's approach and was momentarily distracted. The horse reared, lashed out with a front leg and the hoof raked Dave across the scalp and down one side of his face, opening a gash that bled profusely. Dave chastised the animal with, "You dirty rotten son of a bitch!"

It was in that moment Dave took notice of his father standing on the far side of the corral. Milo removed his black cowboy hat and stood silently for a long moment reshaping that hat, denting it just so with the heel of his hand, pinching the crown, restoring the brim's slight roll. He put the hat back on his head. His jaw muscles bounced rhythmically a time or two and then in a voice very calm and under control he said, "Son, we don't talk like that around here."

Maybe Milo intended to say more, but he did not. He promptly spun on his heels and walked away. Dave stood there, blood flowing freely down his face and dripping onto the dry ground and he thought to himself, "He don't care how much blood I spill; it's just that 'Son, we don't talk like that around here.'" And then, despite his pain, and the blood, Dave laughed.

*****

Except for his time in school, Dave spent most of his growing up years in the hills, riding horses and looking after the cattle and sheep. With lambing season, and driving the sheep to and from summer pasture and general ranch work, Dave typically missed about a third of the school year. When he was in high school he showed a great deal of aptitude in sports, and the coach of the basketball team, Dennis Lacy, went out of his way to make sure Dave attended practices and games. Sometimes Coach Lacy drove to the Franke ranch to help Dave complete his chores, and sometimes he sent team members so Dave would be free to play in an important game.

*****

Dave's introduction to alcohol began when he overheard the high school principal's son bragging that his father kept a bottle of Jack Daniels hidden under the front seat of the family's car. The bottle was there—a full jug—and Dave swiped it and took it home where he shared it with his cousin, Gordon. In addition to being related, the two were best buddies, and even though Gordon was four years older, he and Dave did most everything together; chores, ranching, riding and driving the rural roads of Grant County in Gordon's hotrod Ford coupe. He drove fast and dangerously and when Dave was behind the wheel, he drove the same damn way; barreling across the flats and sliding around tight corners. They made up stories; they were moonshiners outrunning the law, bank robbers driving getaway, escapees on the lam. The two boys were a pair of wild cards; rowdy, taking chances and unmindful of any dangers.

The cousins were known far and wide for their "bear story," a hard-to-believe tale the two concocted so "folks got something to talk about." The story began when herder, Mike Corley, sent word that a big black bear was causing havoc with the Franke's band of sheep on pasture near Greenhorn Mountain.

Dave and Gordon drove to the summer sheep allotment, but by the time they arrived the dirty work was done. Mike Corley had already shot the bear. They wasted no time in loading the 600-pound carcass in the bed of the Franke's pickup, a 1950 Chevrolet, half-ton, green in color with a replaced hood and front fenders painted a distinctive yellow. On the way home the two discussed hunting stories, and on a whim they decided a unique *bear story* of their own was needed. The yarn they fabricated was that Dave, armed with a .22 pistol, was hiking up a draw and jumped the bear. The bear charged and Dave emptied his pistol at the bear but never fazed the bruin. Gordon became the hero. According to the story, he heard the shots from his vantage on a ridge, saw the bear charging Dave, took aim with his 30.30 and killed the bear with a single shot. The bear dropped dead at Dave's feet. That was their story, and the two vowed to stick by it.

On the way through John Day, they stopped at S & M Motors to pick up some needed parts. While they were inside, an old-timer came in and said, "Who's got that ol' yellar and green pickup parked outside?" Dave acknowledged it was his pickup and the old-timer drawled, "Well it's about to bleed to death." Of course the other customers had to see what was causing the pickup to *bleed* and the boys rolled back the tarp, exposing the huge bear. Then they told their *bear story* for the first time.

The bear story was told and retold many times, and when Sunday rolled around Dave and Gordon were in church and listened to Milo retell the story from the pulpit. Although in

Milo's rendition there was a decidedly religious twist, with God intervening, working through Gordon and guiding the unerring shot that killed the bear and saved Dave's life.

*****

Even though his first taste of sour whiskey burned Dave's throat like the pale blue flame from an acetylene torch—the rusty-colored liquid searing a direct line to his stomach—that was forgotten with the rushing sensation as loud as the buzzing of a jar full of angry bees flailing against the glass. Dave lifted the bottle and tried another drink. This time the bite was not as sharp; did not burn with quite the intensity and merely traced a path of warmth to his stomach. As the alcohol hit bottom, Dave detected a curious surge that began in the region of his solar plexus and rushed through his entire body giving him a feeling of unshackled strength, invincibility and boundless energy.

Later that night, when the bottle was empty, Dave was violently sick, vomiting everything in his stomach, then bile and finally he suffered dry heaves and painful convulsions of his stomach muscles. He lay on the ground, tasting and smelling the caustic bitterness. Then he slept or passed out, and upon waking the stars and moon whorled and light played and danced through the bare, gray limbs of a cottonwood tree. He drifted into unsteady sleep once more, and this time upon fully awakening he discovered a new day was breaking soft and low across the broad expanse of eastern sky. Dave had the disconcerting sensation that the bones in his head had been removed and its shape filled with stuffing like some trophy buck. But from the depths of that stuffing, somewhere in the remote recesses of his brain, Dave was remembering—not his misery of being terribly sick or the scream of pain in his pounding head—more the elation and tremendous euphoria, the power and the energy he felt when he was drunk. His body needed more, craved more and demanded more.

27

*****

Charles Denver Melton—he went by Denver—left his home in Laurel County, Kentucky to fight overseas in the European Theatre during the Second World War. The school girls and unmarried women of the area organized a loosely knit group to write letters to the men in uniform, so they could receive news from home and feel as though their war efforts were appreciated. One of the girls who wrote to Denver was Ruby Weaver. Ruby and Denver exchanged many letters, and after the war ended and Denver returned to Laurel County, he was soon courting Ruby. Within a few months they married. As a wedding gift, Denver's father gave the couple a plot of land on the Melton family farm. They built a small home there and Denver tried to be a farmer, but after his travels abroad he found farming to be a confining and solitary existence. He became restless and began talking about following his older brother, Chester, out to Oregon.

Shortly after their daughter Peggy was born—the couple's only child—Denver announced they were moving to Prineville, Oregon where Chester had a service station and had offered Denver a job. Ruby was a submissive and supportive wife, and although it was difficult for her to leave her family and friends in Kentucky, she gave in to Denver and they moved. Even after landing in Prineville, Oregon, Denver's restlessness continued. He worked in his brother's service station for a while and then quit and tried his hand at carpentry, building several duplexes. The Melton family soon moved to Madras where Denver built a store, operated it for a time, sold it and moved the family to Bend where he built and operated a Flying-A Service Station.

Denver abruptly sold that station and bought the Texaco Service Station in Dayville, Oregon, in 1954. He pumped gas and Ruby operated a small sandwich counter in the back of the building. Dayville was an active community of about 250 people; its economy based on logging, sawmill work, ranching and income received from travelers along State Highway 26. The center of social life in the community was the school, the

Pastime Tavern, and the Valley Chapel Church. Even though Ruby Melton had been a devout Southern Baptist, she and her daughter, Peggy, became faithful members of the Valley Chapel Church.

As a child, Peggy thrived in the small town atmosphere. She and her friends hiked, rode bikes and swam in the south fork of the John Day River. In the winter there was sledding and the ponds at the base of Rudio Mountain were flooded and there was ice skating and bonfires to enjoy. But Peggy's real love was horses. She rode at every opportunity when her friends, daughters of ranchers, invited her to spend the night. She begged her father for a horse, but Denver steadfastly refused, claiming he had no use for what he referred to as a *hay burner*.

Denver's brother, Chester, bought the store in Dayville, Dayville Merc, and Denver sold his service station and purchased the Pastime Tavern that adjoined the store. A long porch ran the length of the two businesses and people tended to gather there to visit and gossip. Peggy was allowed to sit on the bench in front of her uncle's store, but was forbidden to come anywhere near the tavern. Denver was very strict about that. The tavern was off limits to Peggy. Denver not only dispensed beer in the Pastime, but also operated an illegal card game in the back room, and if he was not sitting in on a game, the house still made money by taking a rake from each pot.

The drinking and card playing was never mentioned in the Melton home. In fact, Denver lived a separate life from his wife and daughter. Ruby served as the bookkeeper for the Pastime as well as the Dayville Merc, and she cooked at the Dayville School cafeteria. She and her daughter attended every service conducted at the Valley Chapel and Ruby often praised Milo Franke for his fiery sermons and his musical talents; singing and playing the guitar and harmonica. Peggy attended Bible study and then Sunday school, taught by Milo's wife, Evelyn Franke.

Peggy was a willing participant at all the church functions. At the age of eight she had stepped forward at a revival, was baptized, and knelt before the altar and repeated the sinner's prayer. She welcomed Jesus into her heart and dedicated herself to living a godly life.

At that time Dayville was far from a godly town. Jackie Wright, a well-known rodeo cowboy got in a bar fight and his opponent died. Jackie was released into the custody of Milo Franke. And when Manny Martin was shot in the head by his girlfriend's father, the family called for Milo Franke. He went to the hospital and prayed the sinner's prayer with Manny. When the prayer was finished, Manny squeezed Milo's hand, took one final breath and died. Milo was never choosy about who he ministered to. He went where he was needed. He was humble, loving and open-minded—up to a point where it might conflict with his strict interpretation of the teachings in the Bible—and he was a man with an amazing capacity for forgiveness. He became a father figure to Peggy because she seldom saw her own father who was more involved with the elements of sin; drinking, gambling and living a life separate from his wife and daughter.

Traveling evangelists often stayed with the Franke family and ministered on Sundays. One of these traveling evangelists claimed to have the gift of receiving messages directly from God. He began pointing to people in the congregation and asking them to step forward. He loudly proclaimed something that God wanted that particular person to know. One of those he called to participate was a teacher's wife. The teacher was young, handsome, charismatic, and he was having a secret affair with a red-haired, married woman.

The minister laid his hands on the head of the teacher's wife and proclaimed for all to hear, "God is telling me that your heart is broken and bruised by the actions of a red-haired woman. Is that true?"

Peggy was in attendance at the church that day, and she and her girlfriends knew the truth. As the drama unfolded— the minster asked pointed questions and the teacher's wife steadfastly denied any heartbreak caused by a red-headed woman—those who knew the *secret* felt extremely uncomfortable. Peggy learned several valuable lessons in church that day; that Dayville was an extremely small town, eyes were watching, gossip spread quickly, and most people were perfectly capable of adding two and two together and coming up with the truth. After that Sunday, the teacher's wife never returned to church. She and her unfaithful husband remained married, and after the school year ended they quickly moved away. Life in Dayville went on as it always had.

After school and during vacations, Peggy worked as a clerk at her Uncle Chester's grocery store. In her spare time she was an avid reader. After the dinner dishes were washed and after all her homework was done, Peggy faithfully read the Bible, switching to something light and reading just for fun before she fell asleep. She especially loved the writings of Zane Grey and his vivid descriptive abilities; to the point where she could imagine specific locations in the landscape, and the characters in the stories became more like her friends. When she finished a book, she actually felt a tug of longing, wishing the story did not have to end.

Peggy had a deep commitment to her religion and to God. As she was about to begin her freshman year of high school she had the presence of mind to say a prayer and ask God to counsel and guide her in the choices she would make in the coming years related to boys, dating and deciding whom she should consider as a companion in marriage. When it came down to the subject of dating, Denver laid down some hard and fast rules. Peggy was not allowed to ride in a car with any boy. She was not allowed to go on a date unless Denver approved of the boy. And last, but not least, Denver did not want his daughter in the company of a boy unless it was with a group, like at a dance, ball game or a church sponsored event. He was overly protective of his daughter.

Peggy and her friends walked home after school and usually stopped by Jack's Café to indulge themselves with milkshakes and to play the latest music on the juke box. The fall of 1962 the latest dance craze was the *Mashed Potato* and Elvis Presley sang *Return To Sender*. Ray Charles sang *I Can't Stop Loving You*. Pete Seeger sang *Where Have All The Flowers Gone*. The folk trio of Peter, Paul and Mary sang *If I had a Hammer*. Johnny Cash, the Beach Boys and The Beatles were coming of age and kids played the latest rock and roll on 45 rpm vinyl records and drove their own cars back and forth through town on Highway 26, *cruising the gut*.

After sports practices were concluded for the day, the boys joined in the parade through town. They had souped-up engines in their cars and let lake pipes rumble, flipper hubcaps spin and tires squeal as they made noise and showed off. It was a rare event when a Grant County deputy sheriff felt an urge to make a swing through Dayville. The only semblance of law rested with Roy Gray, the slightly unstable and self-proclaimed sheriff of the town. He was in his late 70s and had not an ounce of actual authority to go along with the gold star he so proudly wore on his chest.

One day Roy's tentative mental state simply snapped and he decided to settle an old grudge he held against Ed Chinoth. Ed was coming from the grocery store where he had purchased a quart of ice cream—Rocky Road—and just like in a television western, old Roy Gray stepped into the street with a gun and called Ed Chinoth by name, said something to the effect that Ed had done him wrong and fired a fatal round. According to rumors that quickly circulated, the shooting involved a woman both men had known years before, a woman who caused bad blood between them. Immediately after firing the fatal round, Roy went directly to his nearby house, put the gun to his head and yanked the trigger. He put a yawning hole in the side of his head, but he did not die. He remained hospitalized for a long time and was eventually sent to Pendleton, to the state prison for the criminally insane, where he resided until the day he finally did die.

*****

Dayville was originally settled by a group of Scotch immigrants, and the highlight of each summer was the annual Scotch American Dance and Parade that paid homage to the founders' Scottish heritage. The celebration began with men dressed in kilts and playing bagpipes marching through town while girls dressed in traditional Scottish costumes of tartan skirts and shawls danced in unison. After the parade, a talent contest was held and at its conclusion, Peggy's mom always appeared to escort Peggy home. Peggy was never allowed to attend the community dance where drinking and fistfights were the rule and not the exception. Peggy was sheltered from all that. Her parents made sure of that.

An example of what went on, and what Peggy was protected from, was the Scotch American Dance when Hilmer Martin, a hard drinking rodeo cowboy, got drunk and tried to instigate a fight by asking married women to dance, and then on the dance floor being inappropriate about where he placed his hands. Everyone knew a ruckus was brewing and someone went to tell Hilmer's father, Joe Martin, that his son needed reining in. Joe answered the door barefooted, wearing only his jeans and no shirt. Upon hearing the news, Joe's reaction was to drawl in his slow, typical fashion, "Oh hell, for crying out loud. Can't you boys take care of that?" Then Joe slipped on a shirt, pulled on his slippers and walked over to the Community Hall. He quickly located his son surrounded by a group of angry men. Hilmer had his fists in fighting position and was trying to antagonize someone into taking the first swing. Joe tapped Hilmer on the shoulder, and when his son turned, Joe snapped him on the bridge of the nose. Hilmer's eyes immediately filled with water. Joe twisted one of his son's arms behind his back and drove him home like a plowhorse. The dance resumed with more dancing, drinking and fighting.

*****

Dave Franke was a senior in high school the same year Peggy was a freshman. She knew Dave from having seen him in church. To Peggy it never appeared as though Dave wanted to be at the church where his father was the preacher. Dave was the last one through the door before the service began, and the first to leave when the service concluded. She heard the gossip about Dave; his reputation as a rebel—the James Dean of Dayville he was called—and it was said he drove fast, drank too much at parties where he prided himself at chugging beer, liked to fight and was cutting a wide swath through the eligible girls in the John Day Valley.

Dave was the starting center on the high school basketball team. He was a fierce rebounder and a consistent scorer. The local Friday and Saturday night games brought the ranchers, loggers and mill workers to town. At halftime the men went to the parking lot where they sat on the tailgates of pickup trucks—the beds littered with hay, bailing twine and dogs—and took turns drinking from a communal jug. When the jug was empty, they filed back into the gym, and if play was not going Dayville's way, the men cussed loudly and challenged the referees. Occasionally a fight with spectators from the opposing team broke out in the stands, or on the court. The citizens of Dayville took the game of basketball seriously. If a fight was not settled in the gym, chances are a conclusion would be reached later in the evening in front of the Pastime Tavern.

*****

Once a week the women in town took turns hosting a Bible study group. The first meeting in January, 1963, was scheduled for the Melton home. Evelyn Franke was leading the group when the meeting was interrupted by Dave Franke and his cousin, Gordon. They had stopped to deliver milk—the Franke family sold and delivered whole milk to customers who did not have their own cow—and Ruby invited the boys to stay and have a piece of pie. They readily agreed.

Dave had seen Peggy around; at church, various social functions, and at school. She had always struck him as a gangly little girl. But that night at Bible study, she was different somehow; seemingly overnight Peggy had gone from girl to woman. She seemed confident, laughed easily and often, and did not seem the least bit shy or reserved. Dave took notice.

When the boys left the Bible study it was Gordon who elbowed Dave in the ribs and asked, "Hey, you take a gander at that Melton girl?"

"I seen her," replied Dave coolly.

"For my money she is one good lookin' gal," said Gordon. "I noticed she couldn't seem to keep her eyes off you. She may be a little on the young side, but if I were you I sure as hell wouldn't let that stop me. I don't know why, but she's taken a shine to you."

Whether Gordon was being serious, or only kidding, it never seemed to matter because a fire had been lit inside Dave. He began seeking out Peggy at school, or after church. He talked and flirted with her. One Sunday he told her, "We got horses at the ranch. You ought to come out and go riding sometime." That interested Peggy.

Dave was 18 years old and Peggy was only 14 years old. They were polar opposites in many ways. Peggy was very committed to her religion, and as an only child, she had been sheltered and protected all her life. Dave went out of his way to prove he was against everything his father stood for. He smoked, drank, chewed tobacco, owned a car and drove it fast, and it was said he ran with girls who had even faster reputations. In spite of all that, Peggy found herself drawn to Dave and his status as an outlaw. He was tall and handsome, exciting and challenging, and although her girlfriends warned Peggy, "He's way out of your league," and, "All you'll ever get from Dave Franke is a broken heart," she thought those girls were envious that Dave was directing his attentions toward her.

Dave was determined, ambitious and confident. He loved to break horses, and the secret to his success was in discovering how a horse thinks. A horse has no sense of time. For Dave the breaking process would continue until the horse submitted. If a horse got the idea he could throw a rider he would try. If Dave did get thrown, he got back on. He was an expert at dusting himself off. Dave pursued Peggy with the same mindset as he did when he broke horses. If the wooing of Peggy Melton took days or weeks it did not really matter to Dave. He doggedly pursued Peggy, and she was flattered by his interest in her.

Dave and Peggy's "first date" really was not much of a date at all. Dave simply asked Peggy if he could drive her home after the basketball game. Peggy had to ask her father's permission. Denver thought about it for a long moment before giving his answer. He liked and respected Milo Franke and felt as though he could trust his son. He told Peggy she could ride home from the game with Dave but warned, "If I see that boy driving fast, or hear that he drives fast with you in the car, you won't be riding with him no more." Peggy meekly agreed to her father's conditions.

After the game Dave drove Peggy to Jack's Café and they drank soda pop and talked, and then he took her home. At the top of the steps, as Peggy reached for the door handle, Dave stopped her. He hauled her into a tight embrace and kissed her forehead. It was a sweet kiss, eager but not urgent, and then Dave released her, wished her a good night and walked away. Peggy opened the door and went inside. Her head seemed to be spinning and she was smiling. Her mother asked if she had had a good time and Peggy, still grinning, said, "Yes," and went directly to her room.

Dave knew exactly how to win Peggy's heart. When springtime rolled around he invited her on a moonlight horseback ride. They rode side by side to the top of an exposed ridge. From this vantage they could see out over the countryside; below in the valley were a few electric nightlights delineating the scattered ranches, and the moon and stars were splashed across the great expanse of blue-black sky. Peggy commented, "Isn't it exhilarating and wonderful to be out here and see God's creation all around us?"

Dave was not thinking about the wonders of nature. His only thought was his desire for Peggy. He maneuvered his horse close to the horse Peggy was riding. He leaned toward Peggy and kissed her with such passion that 14-year-old Peggy felt as though she was falling through that star-laden sky, and by the time she had caught her breath, she knew she was hopelessly in love with Dave Franke.

*****

Dave had never had a "steady girlfriend," and had once informed his father he did not need a girlfriend. He said girls were more trouble than they were worth, and said he would be perfectly content if he could ride a good colt and live all alone at Jerry's cabin. And while he rode, Dave often sang to himself, his horse and the countryside he was passing through; usually a tune he learned from one of the neighbors:

> *I've got no use for the women a true one may seldom be found*
>
> *They'll use a man for his money when its gone they'll turn him down*
>
> *They're all alike at the bottom selfish and grasping for all*
>
> *They'll stay by a man when he's winning and laugh in his face when he falls....*

When Milo found out Dave was dating Peggy Melton, a young member of his congregation, he warned his son, "Don't you ever break that little girl's heart, or you will have to answer to me. Do I make myself clear?"

"Perfectly clear," said Dave. He had no intention of doing anything to harm Peggy. He had fallen in love with her.

Dave and Peggy continued to date, and at Dave's high school graduation he gave Peggy his class ring. They were officially *going steady* which meant they were exclusively dating each other. The ring was huge and Peggy had to wrap white athletic tape around the band to keep it on her finger.

Dave took a job working on a construction crew out of town and sometimes, to show his commitment, Dave left Peggy his new car—a sleek, silver 1964, Chevrolet Super Sport with light gray leather interior and four-on-the-floor—for her to drive while he was away. That fall Dave enrolled in college at Treasure Valley Community College, 100 miles away in Ontario, Oregon. The two lovebirds exchanged letters on a regular basis. Dave was a great letter writer, romantic and able to put his feelings into words. Peggy loved that he could do that. They talked on the telephone, a payphone, and they talked as long as Dave had change in his pocket. Peggy later acknowledged it was probably a blessing in disguise that she and Dave were separated by so many miles; especially considering the fact two of her best friends who had steady boyfriends became pregnant while still in high school.

On a warm evening in May, 1966, Peggy graduated with the largest class in the history of Dayville High School. There were 14 graduates and most had attended school in Dayville all 12 years. They were like family, and since their freshman year they had worked at fundraisers—operating the concession stand at ball games, holding car washes, having bake sales and feeding hungry elk and deer hunters during hunting seasons—to raise money for a senior class graduation trip to Disneyland.

Dave attended Peggy's graduation, and he shocked her silly by asking for his ring back. As Peggy was slipping the ring off her finger, tears welling in her eyes, Dave dropped to one knee in front of her, opened a black jewelry box with a diamond ring and said, "I have another ring for you. Will you do me the honor of marrying me and being my wife?"

Peggy squealed, tears of joy ran unabashedly down her pretty cheeks and she exclaimed, "Yes, oh yes, I will, I will!" The two vowed to keep their upcoming marriage a secret until Peggy returned from her senior trip because they wanted their parents to be the first to know and not hear the news through the grapevine.

It was a short graduation night. At 4 a.m. the following morning, 10 seniors, including Peggy, departed from the school parking lot on the senior trip to Disneyland. They were split between two cars; one car driven by Principal Ellis, and the other car by his wife. In addition to being the drivers, the couple would also serve as chaperones. They drove south—taking a side trip to view Crater Lake—and continued on to Reno; and driving all night they crossed the Sierra Nevada Mountain Range and arrived in San Francisco early the following morning. The members of the Dayville High School graduating class rode cable cars, had lunch on Fisherman's Wharf and experienced the unusual sights, sounds and smells of Chinatown, before departing for their Disneyland destination.

The class spent three days and nights in Anaheim. One night the principal allowed the students to take his car, a convertible, and go to a drive-in movie. After the movie the kids drove around with the top down. The hicks from the sticks had come to the big city. At one point, when they were stopped in traffic, one of the boys jumped out, shinnied up a palm tree and threw down a coconut. The carload of kids cheered enthusiastically. They also drove to the beach and reveled in the ocean where the water was so beautiful. They were in California, frolicking on the beach made famous by The Beach Boys. They were living the California dream and went swimming in the Pacific Ocean without knowing anything about outgoing tides. Peggy, a strong swimmer, found herself being pulled out to sea. She panicked and screamed. Several of the boys from her class swam to her aide and towed her to shore.

When Peggy returned from her week-long senior trip, she put on her engagement ring. She and Dave broke the news to Dave's parents. They readily agreed to the marriage. Peggy's parents were also accepting, but made one condition to the proposed marriage, that Peggy follow through on her educational plans to attend Links Business College in Boise, Idaho.

The couple was married in Dayville on September 3, 1966, at the Valley Chapel Church. Milo Franke officiated. It was 104 degrees with no air conditioning in the church. Friends decorated Dave's Super Sport with white shoe polish, placed gravel in the hub caps, slathered Limburger cheese on the manifold and tied tin cans to the back bumper. Dave and Peggy raced out of town and stopped for dinner at The Brand restaurant between Redmond and Bend. They found the 2D brand burned into the wood on a table; the brand belonging to Milo and his brother, Clarence. Milo liked to brag that the brand stood for "two dumbbells."

The first night of their married life was spent at a motel in Bend, and the following day they drove to the Oregon Coast and stayed at Sailor Jack's Motel in Lincoln City. They spent very little time on the beach. Dave, claiming they needed to make up for the three years of "lost time" spent dating, wanted to spend most of their time just *honeymooning*.

Chapter Four

Spring came reluctantly to the Mojave Desert; nights became increasingly warmer, brief rains arrived and flowers appeared in a profusion of colors—red, white, yellow and blue—bloomed and died quickly. During the day Dave drove the dusty roads of Apple Valley checking on his jobs. In the evenings the long shadows of the rugged San Bernardino Mountains—dour stony peaks hammered tightly against the skyline; stone streaked with the muted colors of age—were laid out as a backdrop to the humps of hills. Eruptions of scoured rocks gave the appearance of the wind having ripped away the earth's flesh so its bones lay exposed to view. Above the desolate expanse of landscape, vultures floated in silence, spanning their wings and wafting on the wind in high, tight circles, patiently waiting for something to die—for Dave to die—but he remained busy with his various construction projects and took no notice. After the brief rains had ended, the only moisture the desert plants received was a faint mist of dew that gathered on veined leaves each night, and the thin sheen was gone as soon as the rays of the climbing sun touched them. Dave was oblivious to all that, just as he was unaware of the circling vultures.

Dave was the general contractor for a giant warehouse nearing completion; the walls were standing tall and the crew was busy getting ready for the arrival of the trusses. Other building projects Dave had in the works, scattered around Apple Valley, were in various stages of completion and required Dave's constant attention. Dave should have been happy; he was working hard and had the potential to make a good profit, but his life remained an absolute mess. He felt the weight of responsibility; and he felt the humiliation for abandoning his family and leaving Peggy to face the hounding of the many creditors. He left her with the relentless assault of the IRS demanding taxes that grew by the day with their damnable interest and penalties.

Sometimes Dave had vivid dreams of Oregon. He imagined the fields burly and flush with growing alfalfa, smelled the tang of sage, saw the turquoise sheen of the John Day River in the shimmer of summer's sun, felt the feathery touch of a soft sigh of wind braiding and unbraiding itself as it tickled the pines. He recalled trips to the rocky Oregon Coast where he appreciated the urgent lapping rhythm of the waves, the playful call of the gulls and the unfamiliar smells that floated up from the depths of the Pacific Ocean. Invariably, as memories raged, he awoke to tears wetting his cheeks. Stranded as he was on the Mojave Desert, he felt just as trapped as a man convicted and sentenced to life on death row; trapped in a prison of his own making. He wiped at his tears and runny nose with the sleeve of his shirt, eased to his knees and said a quick prayer his misery would end—one way or another—his misery would just come to an end.

It had been months since Dave had seen his family and that was probably for the best. He was drinking even more than he ever had. He despised his weakness, but unless he drank, he lay awake in his trailer, homesick, his heart aching for his family, thinking about everything that had gone wrong and wallowing in his unhappiness. So he drank to dull his pain and when he did sleep it was in quick fits and starts. The voice, he kept hearing that damned voice threatening to have him at forty. He had only a couple more months to go and then his 41st birthday would roll around and that menacing prophesy would prove unfounded. He was so obsessed with the upcoming event that he had tacked a calendar to a cupboard door in his trailer and took delight in crossing off each day with a red felt marker. He counted the days until his birthday. He worked, waited, and drank.

Dave loathed himself for his drinking, and yet he was powerless to stop. When he returned to the trailer he always poured a brimming glass of Black Velvet, and when that was gone he poured another, and another after that until, laying on the couch with his Army surplus sleeping bag pulled to his shoulders, he slipped into the black void of unconsciousness. Each morning, when he awoke and took his first drink of alcohol—the first drink of the day was the best, the one to savor, all the others were only chasing that memory—he would again chastise himself, knowing this was no way for a man to live. But this was Dave's life, and he supposed, since he lived like an animal, perhaps he should feel no more than an animal feels—heat, cold, hunger, fatigue—and those emotions felt by humans—love, regret, sorrow, unhappiness, grief and loneliness—would no longer be of consequence.

*****

After Dave and Peggy were married they moved to Boise so Peggy could attend Link's Business College. Peggy's folks had previously moved to Boise, and the couple lived with Denver and Ruby until Dave found employment at the OK Tire Store and they could afford an apartment. Dave, burning with ambition to make his mark in the world, said the tire shop was a dead-end job. If he were to stay, he claimed he would be throwing away their future. Dave's brother, Don, suggested Dave contact Bob Coats, an engaging young man from Bend, Oregon, an engineer and a true entrepreneur who was just getting started in the construction business. Coats hired Dave over the phone and assigned him to a D-4 Cat cleaning roadways. After a few months, Dave was switched to rebuilding bridges near Dayville damaged in the '64 flood: one on Mountain Creek and the other the main Highway 26 bridge in Dayville. During this time Peggy remained in Boise, living with her parents and finishing her schooling.

Bob Coats hired Dave to serve as his paving crew foreman—Coats owned a Ready Mix plant in Bend—and Dave took the job even though he knew very little about paving. He was only 21 years old, but considered himself a quick learner and figured he could easily learn what he needed to know while working on the job. He had no reservations about running a crew of men. His theory was, if he worked hard and his men saw that, they would work equally as hard.

Peggy graduated from Link's Business College and she and Dave moved into a rental house in Bend. Even though Dave worked long hours as foreman of the paving crew, he got it in his mind he could build a house, reasoning he and Peggy would not have to pay rent and they could build equity in a place of their own. After all, Milo had built several churches and Dave believed he was perfectly capable of building a house. He knew, since he and Peggy had very little in savings, a building loan would be required. One afternoon he took off early from work and stopped by Equitable Savings and Loan, on Wall Street in downtown Bend. He spoke to the loan officer, a young man wearing a suit and tie. Dave said he was interested in building a house and needed to borrow about $18,000. The loan officer asked a few questions, filled out a one-page application, and told Dave he had the loan and could start building immediately. Dave left the bank not knowing whether to be thankful, or to be just plain scared for assuming such a huge debt on what he suddenly viewed as a risky venture.

Dave bought a lot across the street from where they were living and went to work building a 1,200-square-foot house. A contractor was building a spec house nearby, and after the crew went home, Dave looked around at what had been accomplished that day to get an idea of what he needed to do next. He did all the carpentry work, including hanging sheetrock, texturing, painting and even building cabinets and laying carpet. Dave and Peggy moved into the house, but were only there a few months before they had an offer and sold the house, making what they thought was a windfall profit.

With the first house behind him, and the result having been so lucrative, Dave decided maybe he should build a couple more houses. His plan was, after working on the paving crew all day, he could build houses in the evenings and on weekends.

While paving the driveway for a man who owned a small subdivision on Bear Creek Road, Dave mentioned he might be in the market for a lot or two. He purchased two lots from the customer, obtained building loans and went to work. One house sold before Dave had even finished it, the other was sold within a few weeks of tacking up a for sale sign. From the two homes a net profit of $20,000 was realized.

One day Dave was busy with his day job, paving near La Pine, when Bob Coats pulled up in his pickup, got out and walked over to Dave. Wasting no words he said, "Understand you've gone into building homes."

"On my own time," said Dave defensively.

"Today might be a good day for you to build houses full time," said Coats and he turned away. As he opened the door to his pickup he told Dave, "Swing by the office. Your last check will be ready for you."

Dave did not know how he was going to break the news to Peggy, that Bob Coats had fired him, but he also had confidence he could make an excellent living building and selling homes. He was not sure about the timing though. He had wanted to stretch things out—keep working for Coats and drawing a steady paycheck—while growing his construction business on the side. Now it was all or nothing.

If Peggy was afraid, she never showed that fear to Dave. She was supportive and encouraging, saying she knew Dave could make a go of his construction dream. Dave said he was hesitant about taking such a risk when they did not have a safety net of savings. Peggy assured him she had taken the profit from the houses he had built, and had a substantial nest egg. She said it would see them through until the houses he was going to build were sold.

*****

Dave and Peggy were lying in bed, discussing their day, when Dave got off on a tangent and started talking about his little sister who was eight years younger than he was, and how she had been so sick and colicky as a baby. He said, "She cried and screamed and it was horrible. I don't know why anyone would want to have kids."

Peggy had just gone off birth control pills—the side effects were making her ill—and besides, she wanted to get pregnant and start a family. She was upset with Dave and what she perceived as his not wanting children. She rolled to the far side of the bed, turned her back to Dave and sniffled quietly into her pillow.

"What's wrong? Did I say something I shouldn't have said?" asked Dave. He scooted close to Peggy and rested a hand on the curve of her hip.

She pushed his hand away. "You don't ever want children," she said, slinging the accusation in Dave's direction, and began to cry.

"For Pete sake, I never said anything of the kind," said Dave. "All I said was I don't know how a parent could stand to have a colicky kid. I never thought about having kids of our own. If you want a baby, why waste time? Let's get with the program." With brute force Dave yanked Peggy into his arms and began kissing away her tears. Before long she was laughing and returning his kisses.

That was the extent of Dave and Peggy's *family planning talk* and by August Peggy was suffering with morning sickness that oftentimes lasted most of the day. On March 4, 1969, after a difficult delivery, Marlece Shannon Franke was born. Peggy and the baby were kept in the hospital for four days. The doctor said he would release them at 11 a.m. on Saturday. Peggy was excited to be able to go home and show off her baby to family, friends and neighbors. She got out of bed, put on a pretty dress, did her hair and makeup, even slipped into a pair of fancy heels she had thought to pack for the occasion. She dressed her baby in an adorable outfit and she waited. And she waited some more. It was not until nearly 2 p.m. that Dave came dragging into the hospital. His eyes were red-rimmed and swollen, and he looked like he was suffering from a severe hangover.

"Where have you been?" demanded Peggy.

"My brothers stopped over and we celebrated the baby; guess we celebrated a bit too much," apologized Dave. He shrugged his husky shoulders, a gesture full of resignation and fatigue, and sheepishly admitted, "I overslept."

Even though Dave and his late-night partying had taken away some of Peggy's joy, she readily accepted Dave's excuse. What could she say? What could she do? She did not like confrontation. She was never going to change Dave. When they arrived at their home, Dave opened the door for her, and Peggy made nice and handed him his baby daughter to carry inside.

*****

Chuck Boardman, a well-respected, retired attorney in Bend, the former Deschutes County District Attorney and former Municipal Judge, called and asked to talk to Dave.

"Can you find the old dairy off Bear Creek Road?" asked Chuck, a man of few words.

"Sure," replied Dave. "I'm familiar with that area."

"Meet me there," said Chuck. "I'll be driving my blue pickup." He hung up the receiver and the line went dead.

Dave laughed and told Peggy, "You won't believe what just happened. Chuck Boardman wants to meet me at the old dairy on Bear Creek. I heard he's trying to get a subdivision going out there. I think he wants to talk business."

As Dave drove onto the old dairy property he spotted an old blue pickup truck—1956, three-quarter ton, long box— and standing beside it was Chuck Boardman, dressed in a suit and tie and wearing a pair of gum boots with his slacks tucked inside. Dave got out of his rig, approached Chuck and introduced himself.

"I know who you are," said Chuck. He shook Dave's hand, walked to the passenger side of his pickup, got in and directed Dave, "You drive."

Dave got behind the wheel. He started the truck and asked, "Where do you want to go?"

"Just drive around a bit," said Chuck.

Dave drove the muddy roads, trails really, that had recently been punched across the virgin landscape with a D-6 Cat. The blue truck weaved between two- and five-acre parcels that Chuck had laid out in his Dobbin Acres subdivision. That day a fresh storm was moving into Central Oregon, and off to the west, dark, roily clouds broke against the snowy flanks of the Three Sisters Mountains and worked valiantly to bury a patch of blue sky. Frosty moisture began to fall, not as flakes, nor rain, but as tiny white wads that landed and froze in a thin glaze atop the scars of newly turned soil. Wind rattled the trees, shook limb against limb that made wild tapping noises; and when a shaking limb gave up and split from the trunk, it landed below on the cold ground with a noise like a final grunt.

Tucked in the cab of the awkwardly lurching truck, the men remained silent; and the audible noises were the howl of the wind, the whirr of the heater and the grumblings of motor, gears and windshield wipers.

Chuck turned toward Dave, raised his voice to be heard over the cacophony of sound and asked, "How many you want?"

Dave horsed the truck around a near 90 degree corner, the rear wheels sliding, and answered, "I don't have the money to buy into your subdivision."

"I didn't ask if you had the money," replied Chuck. "I asked how many lots you want."

"One," said Dave. "One will do me for a while."

A few days later, Dave received the signed deeds to all 30 parcels in the Dobbin Acres subdivision. On each deed was the price that Chuck wanted when the property had been built on and was sold. Dave stood holding the deeds in his hands and told Peggy, "Chuck must be getting senile. He deeded me his entire subdivision, and we don't owe a dime until the property is sold."

Dave went to Chuck's office, and when he walked in Chuck was sitting behind his massive wooden desk, feet casually resting on one corner. He was busy holding his tie with one hand while leaning far to one side to spit a long string of tobacco juice into a gallon coffee can sitting on the floor.

"You made a mistake," said Dave. "You sent me all the deeds to your subdivision, not just one."

"No mistake," replied Chuck, backhanding his lips with his hand. "Use the land as collateral, build a house, sell it and pay me the price I ask for."

"That's a lot of houses for me to build," said Dave.

"You'll do just fine," said Chuck. He spit again and concluded, "You best get busy. Remember, you've got a lot of houses to build."

"Why me?" asked Dave.

"I checked you out," said Chuck. "I know I can trust you. You've got the ambition to get the job done."

Dave soon discovered that Chuck had never completed the legal requirements to have Dobbin Acres recognized as an approved subdivision. Chuck even admitted it was illegal, but he was well-versed in law and knew all the loopholes. He bullied his subdivision through the chain of governmental bodies and Dave built all 30 homes, selling many of them before they were completed. Both men made money, and they went in as partners on an office complex that Dave built at First and Penn in the Bend Industrial Complex.

*****

One of Dave's subcontractors introduced Dave to George Whitney, the potentate of the Shrine Arcade Temple in Portland and a very successful real estate developer. George informed Dave that Farm Home Administration was becoming very active in loaning money for rural developments and made Dave an offer, "I will do all the legwork with Farm Home, purchase buildable lots in small towns all around the state, and I want you to be the general contractor, overseeing the building of homes. I'll pay all the bills and as soon as you complete a home—1,100-square-foot, same plan over and over again—your projected profit will be around $5,000. It's a can't miss opportunity. What do you say?"

The offer caught Dave off guard. He told George he would have to think about it and discuss it with Peggy. By then he and Peggy had added two more daughters to their growing family, and if Dave took the job, it would require that he be gone from home on extended trips to oversee the building projects. Based on his success with Chuck Boardman, Dave was being sought out and wooed by other developers and investors who had money to feed into the Bend building boom. In reality, Dave knew he would never have to leave Bend and could stay as busy as he wanted to be. But in the end, Dave made the decision he could do it all; continue to build his construction business in Bend while taking on the Farm Home Administration projects in towns scattered throughout Oregon: Pilot Rock, Athena, Pendleton, Arlington, Condon, Fossil, Bly, Metolius, Merrill, Prairie City, John Day and Mount Vernon.

During this hectic time, Dave began relying on alcohol as a crutch. Drinking gave him seemingly endless energy, and he needed that. Alcohol allowed him to be more sociable and gregarious and more outgoing than was his nature. And it gave him courage, nerve and guts. He told himself, if his drinking ever became a problem, he could always quit. But in his estimation it never became a problem. He started drinking when he was away from home, and when he was home he hid his drinking from Peggy and the girls.

In other parts of the country the housing market had begun showing signs of faltering, but in Bend, except for a few hiccups and foreclosures, the building boom continued to roll along and Dave rode the crest of that wave.

*****

A representative of a mortgage company in Salem called Dave at his office and said the mortgage company had financed Clear Sky subdivision in Bend, but the original investor had made bad financial decisions, gone broke and the mortgage company had been forced to take over the subdivision. The representative said there were 115 buildable home lots and 20 duplex lots in the subdivision. He asked Dave if he would be interested in taking over the development.

Dave was aware of the problems with the Clear Sky subdivision, and yet he was brash enough to think he could solve those problems. He took a drink of Black Velvet, thought for a quick moment, and told the representative of the mortgage company, "I can do it. Set up the building loans, and I'll get to work."

The main hurdle to building in the Clear Sky subdivision was that the City of Bend had agreed to extend sewer lines, but it would be at least a couple years before those lines could be completed. Without sewer, no building permits would be issued. Dave leaped that hurdle by installing two huge underground tanks to be used as settling ponds. The sewage would be pumped and hauled away until the City of Bend could extend the lines.

Dave went to work building homes and duplexes. He established his own real estate company, Stagecoach Realty, to sell the homes. At a selling price of $40,000, the homes sold faster than Dave could have his crews of subcontractors build them.

*****

During this time, Peggy continued to keep the books on the diverse projects that Dave was involved in, marveling at his boundless energy. They now had four daughters, lived in a nice home and Peggy had a brand new Oldsmobile Toronado to drive. She had every material thing she needed or wanted, but rarely saw Dave. He was at the office, traveling to check on the Farm Home Administration projects, just busy like a juggler who starts spinning plates on sticks and has to constantly run from one to the next to keep them all spinning. She really did not notice Dave's drinking because she was so involved with business and family. She still viewed the relationship she had with Dave as an extension of when they were first married. Back then they joked they were like Bonnie and Clyde, the two of them against the world.

*****

Oren Reed—the Reeds were one of the most prominent families in Bend—approached Dave about taking over his Desert Woods subdivision, a sprawling development that included several hundred buildable lots. Dave was not sure he could take on yet another major project, especially since the recession seemed to be reaching the Bend market making investment more risky and volatile. But in the end he agreed to take 25 and see how that went before committing to another 25 lots.

When Dave approached Ernie Miller at Mortgage Ban Corporation, the Salem based company which had sold and financed Dave on the Clear Sky subdivision, the banker was only too eager to finance the Desert Woods subdivision. With the financing in hand, Dave began building homes. The first 25 lots were built and sold. Another 25 lots were built and sold. Dave bought the Chalet Motel on the south side of Bend. He built a 100,000-square-foot warehouse. He built and began operating the 35,000-square-foot Central Oregon Sports Center. He bought the ranch in Powell Butte, built a custom home and moved his family there. He bought the Franke ranch in Dayville. He was wheeling and dealing and it all seemed as though he was playing a spirited game of Monopoly. Money came in; money went out. It was nothing but Monopoly money and life was a thrill a minute.

*****

There was an end to the roller coaster ride of the building boom in the Bend market. Since taking over Clear Sky subdivision, and resurrecting the failed company, Dave had always financed his numerous construction projects through Ernie Miller's Mortgage Ban Corporation, a company that Ernie's father had started as a loan institution back in the days after the Great Depression. Dave was operating on a 10 million dollar loan from Mortgage Ban Corporation and his construction business had reached the point where, every month, it took a million dollar draw to pay his many subcontractors. Dave always made it a point to travel to Salem with the paperwork in hand to make his draw. Usually Peggy went along to answer any specific questions that Dave might not know. He knew the big picture, he made the decisions, but he never knew the details. Sometimes Peggy arranged for a babysitter and then she and Dave could run over to the Oregon Coast for a night's vacation, and if they were lucky they might be able to stretch the vacation into an entire weekend.

The day came when they walked into Mortgage Ban Corporation and were told that the owner, Ernie Miller, wanted to see them upstairs in his office. Ernie was a big man, six-foot-five or six-foot-six. He was seated behind his oak desk. Stacks of white papers were arranged around him in artful piles. Ernie did not stand or extend his hand. He merely sat looking morose and worried.

Dave and Peggy sat down. Ernie looked up at Dave, and without bothering with small talk he admitted, "I'm out of money."

Dave, thinking Ernie was joking, caught himself smiling. But Ernie did not break into a laugh, or even a good-old-boy grin. He just sat there with his same rigid posture and a blank expression of resignation on his face.

"You can't be," said Dave. He felt a knot in his gut torque tighter. Damn he needed a drink. "I've made you millions. Where did it all go?"

"It's gone," said Ernie.

"How can I make my draw?" asked Dave.

"You can't," said Ernie.

"Ernie," said Dave, "Do you expect me to go home and tell my subs there's no money to pay them? I can't do that."

Ernie's spirits seemed to brighten just a little. He said, "I've got an idea that might—in the short-term at least—save us both. We go over to Aladdin Bush Bank. I have all your financials and you look good on paper. I think you can borrow a million dollars from them. You loan it to me. I give you your draw."

"Is that legal?" asked Dave.

"Absolutely," replied Ernie.

"Why will they loan me a million dollars? They don't know me," said Dave.

"They know me," said Ernie.

Ernie, Dave and Peggy walked across the street to the Aladdin Bush Bank. They went directly to the manager's office. Introductions were made and Ernie got down to business, saying Dave was in need of a short-term loan of a million dollars.

"Why don't *you* loan him the money?" the manager asked Ernie.

"I don't have it, not at this moment I don't," said Ernie.

The manager turned to Dave and asked what he had for collateral. Dave replied, "Nothing."

At that point Ernie produced the necessary financial paperwork and explained that Dave was a Bend developer and stated he needed the million dollars to pay his subcontractors. He clarified that it would be a short-term loan for five days or less. And Ernie promised to personally guarantee the loan.

"One question," said the banker. He addressed Ernie, "Is Mr. Franke a trustworthy individual?" He tipped his head in Dave's direction.

"Absolutely," said Ernie.

"You can have your million dollars, Mr. Franke," said the manager.

Dave took the million dollar cashier's check from Aladdin Bush Bank and loaned the money to Mortgage Ban Corporation. The draw was issued. Three days later, Ernie was able to gather the necessary funds and repay the loan to Aladdin Bush Bank. Even after this incident, Dave still failed to see the handwriting on the wall.

As it turned out, this was the beginning of the end for Ernie Miller. He had made bad loans, loans without adequate collateral, and he lost his family business. He was a Catholic, and the one thing he wanted to accomplish in his lifetime was to visit Vatican City. He got his wish. It was his last wish. While viewing Vatican City he suffered a massive heart attack and died on the floor of the Sistine Chapel.

*****

The deadly heat of the Mojave Desert was broken by a blue-black wall of clouds that appeared out of the western reaches and spread a greenish cast over the parched land. Electricity filled the air. Soundless lightning flashed far away. A warm wind sprang to life, blowing sand around. The humidity was suffocating. The devil was doing his best to make the ground sour and steamy, and the air was ripping mad.

Dave stepped out of his pickup and into the maelstrom of weather. A few slanting raindrops slapped his face. It was hard to tell the raindrops from his tears. Gone was the swagger of a man who thought he could do everything, anything. That swagger had been replaced by the shuffle of a beaten prizefighter, out on his feet, staggering, trying to reach his corner before he collapsed.

Dave opened the door and stepped inside his trailer. The mirror was in front of him, but he avoided it as he always did. If he caught his reflection it seemed as though his eyes went inside to a depth he found uncomfortable, as though the eyes, without asking his permission, helped themselves to anything they wanted, and that was unnerving. The few times it did happen, Dave felt shame, deadness and a longing for family and all that was being denied him. Warring emotions fought for control. He poured a drink. The Black Velvet altered his mood slightly, mollifying the pain but stimulating the shame.

The storm blew over and the sun set, the sky turned dark and threatening; the moon and stars appeared glittering momentarily like chips of reflective ice, and then disappeared under a sullen barrage of eggshell colored clouds. The wind returned to push warm air around the desert. By then Dave was on his third drink. The booze had worked to loosen his skin and his face sat fleshy, relaxed and hanging low on his skull. Catching his attention was the shotgun, standing tall over by the door. Why the hell had he brought it? Hunting opportunities? Not likely. Protection, possibly; or was the real reason much more dreadful and ominous?

Dave was well-versed in weapons. He knew a bullet fired from a rifle, doomed by aim to unerringly seek its target, leaves the barrel with exit marks unique to the gun which fired it. It can be traced like a fingerprint can be traced. Ballistic experts can compare a bullet against the grooves inside the barrel and say, conclusively, which rifle fired a particular bullet. With a shotgun, the firing pin ignites a primer that in turn ignites a load of black powder, sending wadding and steel shot into a precise pattern, a killing pattern, an untraceable pattern. At close range a shotgun possesses more lethal power than a rifle. Dave knew that. He tugged the sleeping bag up around his shoulders, laid back on the couch and tried to sleep while the confusing wind huffed and puffed and a wincing rain came down and pinged against the tin roof of the trailer. Dave's last thought was an absurd memory of something he once read in a newspaper about a professor at the University of

Oregon—a French professor if memory served him right— who had committed suicide. That in itself was perplexing. Not perplexing that a professor of French would kill himself, but it was the manner in which he accomplished the deed. He tied a boat anchor around his neck and jumped into Dexter Reservoir. It goes to show, if a man wants to die, he will always find a way to die.

*****

Dave always told himself he would be happy, perfectly content, if he could just spend his days doing those things a cowboy does; ride, calve, doctor, feed, turnout, gather.... Maybe that was true, at least for one side of his personality, but another side caused him to burn with ambition. He wanted to make something of himself, wanted to impress his father, wanted to show everyone he had the courage and determination—and the smarts—to set the business world on fire. More than anything, Dave sought respect.

When Milo and his brother and partner, Clarence, wanted to sell the Franke home ranch out of Dayville, Dave thought he could buy the ranch with the money he was making in construction; and that way he could cowboy on the side. He bought the ranch even though it was running more debt than cattle. The day Peggy was called to Travelers Insurance, the lending institution, to affix her name to the myriad of legal papers that constituted the legal contract to purchase the ranch, she hesitated in the signing. "I'm going to regret this," she told herself, knowing the ranch would take an enormous amount of operating capital and steal even more of Dave's time. They were placing their future at risk; she knew that. Why? Because Dave had his heart set on the ranch and he was such a good salesman he convinced her that this was something they *had* to do. That was the reason they were buying the ranch; they *had* to buy the ranch.

In the back of her mind Peggy heard Dave saying, "We're Bonnie and Clyde. We can do this. Have I ever steered you wrong? How could we fail? We've never failed at anything in our lives. We can do this, Bonnie." Peggy signed her name to the documents.

Dave's brother, Don, became a partner and the ranch manager, while Dave was rarely able to steal time to cowboy. He was kept busy on his many construction projects, scattered all over the state of Oregon, and feeding an enormous amount of money into the ranch to pay the unpaid bills that came with the property.

*****

Dave had a temper, and the trigger to igniting that temper was anyone who dared stand in his way. That trigger became a hair-pull when he was drinking; and away from home, working construction, or at the ranch, he was usually drinking. He had a pint of Black Velvet tucked in his vest pocket the day at the ranch when they were separating yearling steers. The steers were already sold and a truck was backing into position at the chute to load the cattle. The driver, a big man—red beard and shaggy hair—climbed onto the chute rails and waved his arms, redirecting the steers that Dave, on horseback, was attempting to push into the narrow opening.

"I ain't haulin' no cattle 'til I get a check for the haul," announced the big man.

Dave was mad and it showed in the redness of his face and the hard set of his jaw. He growled, "You'll get your goddamned check on the other end. We're loading. Get the hell away from there."

The big man flashed a menacing grin and snapped, "Bullshit. You'll give me a check now."

As fast as a calf roper at the rodeo, Dave fashioned a loop with his lariat and threw an unerring strike, the rope settling over the man's neck like a noose. Dave jerked up the slack and his horse, trained to keep the rope taut, shuffled backwards.

The big man—both hands on the rope, trying to ease the strain on his neck—managed to choke out. "I'll haul your cattle, mister."

"Thought you would change your mind," said Dave as he moved his horse forward. The tension eased, the driver slipped the rope off his neck and scurried away. Dave began pushing steers up the chute and forcing them into the trailer.

*****

Milo understood his son's many sacrifices; the time the ranch took, as well as the money required to pay off the enormous debt load that came with the ranch, but Milo's brother and partner on the ranch, Clarence, never did. He kept taking Dave to court claiming he was owed the money he had invested in the ranch over the years. In every instance the court sided with Dave. But still it cost hundreds of thousands of dollars in attorney fees for Dave to defend himself against his uncle's outlandish lawsuits.

After the fourth unsuccessful court case, Dave told his uncle, "Clarence, I don't want you to take me to court any more. Since you are a minister let's arrange a meeting with the district council of the Assembly of God Church in Salem. You tell them your side. I'll tell them mine. They can make the decision as to who is right. If they side with you and say I owe you money, I'll pay it. But you have to be willing to abide by their decision and stop suing me."

Clarence agreed. They appeared before the district council. Dave had been drinking heavily the night before and was suffering from a hangover and yet he presented his side clearly and concisely, pacing back and forth in front of the assembly. He detailed what the ranch had cost him; in cash, unpaid bills and having to constantly defend himself in court against his uncle. At the conclusion of his remarks, Dave left the room, throwing over his shoulder as he departed, "I've already heard what Clarence has to say. I don't need to hear it again. I've got work to do. You decide whatever you want to decide—just let me know and I'll abide by your decision."

Two days later Dave was notified that the tribunal had made its collective decision. Dave did not owe Clarence anything. Although Dave should have felt a sense of relief, it was hard for him to acknowledge anything but anger; anger at his uncle for dragging him through this mess, anger that it had cost him so much financially, anger at having to deal with it over and over again and still there was bad blood in the family.

*****

Dave had been working hard trying to keep the last vestige of his floundering construction company afloat. He had Farm Home Administration building projects going around the state and was in the process of making a wide swing through Condon, Fossil, Arlington, Pilot Rock, Athena, Pendleton, Prairie City, John Day and Mount Vernon to check on the progress of the projects. Where the jobs were lagging behind, Dave called out the subcontractors and chewed their butts, demanding they do whatever needed to be done in order to get back on schedule. He accepted no excuses. He was drinking hard and bossing men who did not want to be bossed. Dave got his way—he always did—or he fired the subs and brought in others to do the work. It was as simple as that.

The first stop on Dave's swing through the eastern part of Oregon was in the tiny town of Maupin where Dave had subcontractors building several homes under the umbrella of the Farm Home Administration. A Wasco County building inspector had written Dave up on several minor infractions—Dave called them *chicken shit citations*—and when the inspector walked onto Dave's jobsite with his boss, Dave was looking for any excuse to put the inspector in his place. The inspector stepped over to the corner post that held the pink permit and he flipped the plastic pole, knocking the permit onto the ground.

Dave turned to the inspector's boss and said, "He shouldn't have done that, should he?"

"No, he shouldn't have done that," confirmed the boss.

Dave's right hand flashed so fast it was a blur of motion. His tight fist caught the inspector on the point of the chin and he dropped like a pumpkin falling from the back of a speeding truck. The man, with a shocked disbelieving look, landed brusquely on the seat of his pants.

"Don't do that again," admonished Dave. He walked away. Seven more houses were inspected that day and not a single citation was issued.

*****

Dave arrived in Pendleton to find his crew of subcontractors drinking the night away at the lounge in the Red Lion Motel. The lounge was the fanciest in town. Dave bought several rounds and then called the bartender to the far end of the bar and asked, "Between now and closing time, how much money will you make?"

"I don't know," said the bartender, "maybe three or four hundred."

Dave peeled five crisp bills off a roll like they were green leaves off an artichoke and laid them flat on the bar. He said, "I want my men sober and ready for work first thing in the morning. Take the night off. Close early." Dave started to put his money away and changed his mind. He added, "You got some fine looking gals hustling drinks in this bar, but you dress them like a pack of nuns. I want you to buy some outfits that show off their assets, if you get my drift. The next time I come through they better look like Playboy Bunnies." Dave laid a thousand dollars on the bar.

The last stop on Dave's wide swing was the town of Mt. Vernon. After checking on the jobsite he stopped at the liquor store, bought another half-gallon of Black Velvet and headed for home feeling a sense of relief that the grueling trip was almost over. Even though he would arrive home late, he could sleep in his own bed and be with his wife. He passed through Dayville and then Mitchell and kept driving, sipping the miles away from the jug he kept on the seat beside him. He went up and over the mountains at Ochoco Summit and was unaware of time or distance. It was night, full dark, a time when a drinking man might forget where he is going or why he is going there. Dave started to feel that there was nothing connecting him to anything else. He finally passed out.

When Dave awoke a red light was throbbing on the far side of his eyelids. He opened his eyes. Everything around him was strange and vague, except for the overhead light in the center of his windshield that was blinking red. He remembered being on the highway driving from Mitchell, and as he looked around it slowly dawned on him that he was stopped for the one traffic light in the town of Prineville. He was at Third and Main, in front of where the old Ochoco Inn had once stood before it burned to the ground in 1966. He remembered seeing the landmark hotel that looked for all the world like a Spanish hacienda; had seen it many times in the past.

The red flashed on. The red flashed off. The red flashed on.

Dave's pickup—the motor running, the truck out of gear—was parked with the front end protruding into the intersection. There was no traffic. And Dave did not know how he had arrived at this point, nor how long he might have been sitting there with the truck idling. Two minutes? Two hours? Dave checked the rearview mirror to make sure there was no one behind him, especially not a cop. The coast was clear. He shoved the bottle of Black Velvet under his seat, kicked the pickup into gear and eased forward on his way home.

*****

When Dave first moved to Apple Valley he had contemplated taking his favorite horse, Goliath, with him. But there was no pasture for the horse, no time to ride, and he had quickly given up on the idea. Goliath was a powerful horse—17 hands at the withers—with a great disposition, an aptitude for working cattle and he possessed the surefootedness of a mountain goat in the hills. When on the move, Goliath was constantly searching for hazards with his large, dark eyes and tasting the wind with his wide, open nostrils. He had power and stamina, and to Dave he was more than a horse; he was a companion, a thrill to be astride and to feel the slap of the world as he galloped until he was hot and lathered. Dave preferred a flashy horse because he was so sure of his abilities in the saddle he knew he could handle a showoff horse.

Goliath remained on the Powell Butte ranch and one morning, as the girls were hurrying to catch the school bus, they came upon a ghastly sight at the head of the lane. Goliath had attempted to cross the metal cattle guard, had fallen through and broken both his front legs. In pain and agony he was making pitiful sounds, showing white around his frightened eyes and foaming at the mouth. The girls raced home to tell their mother this devastating news.

A neighbor came by and promptly sent Peggy and the girls back to the house. Peggy turned up the radio so the girls would not hear the report of the rifle when the neighbor shot Goliath, or hear the whine of the backhoe as it drug away the body and buried it. Peggy, who had endured so much in the past—dissolving Franke Construction Inc., going through bankruptcy, fighting a lengthy battle with the IRS, and on a daily basis having to answer to the multitude of bill collectors she could not pay—was not at all sure she could endure this latest trauma. She fell to her knees and prayed. She prayed for Goliath. She prayed that somehow, some way, her grief might be lifted. And she prayed for God to give her the necessary strength to tell Dave what had happened to his favorite horse.

For all of Peggy's resolve, when Dave did call, she quickly faltered and fell into an abyss of blubbering emotions. Dave misread what she was trying to tell him, and at first thought one of his daughters had been severely injured or killed. Peggy finally managed to get across what had happened. The news hit Dave hard and he tried to imagine Goliath trapped in the cattle guard, legs broken, suffering. The image he conjured was too brutal for Dave to endure and he abruptly shoved the disturbing images from his mind.

"I can hear you breathing," Peggy finally said. "I know you're still there. Will you talk to me?"

Peggy was worried about Dave and his reaction to this harrowing event, but except for the sound of Dave's irregular deep and dry breathing, there was near silence on the line. Dave put his hand over the mouthpiece, and then there was only the steady hiss denoting the miles of separation. Silence could no more be read than blank pages in a book, and when Dave came to that realization, he placed the receiver on the cradle so slowly and delicately that Peggy never knew the exact moment when he was gone.

For a long time Dave stood inside the phone booth, on the corner in front of the highway lounge in Apple Valley, the door propped open with his foot, and all he could do was cry. He stood in the darkness, the occasional car whizzing past on its hurried way to Las Vegas or Los Angeles, and he thought about his horse and everything else that had gone wrong in his life. He concluded life was like a goddamned card game. He thought how we are all dealt a specific hand. Some people get nothing but face cards, and are dealt pairs, triplets, straits, flushes and four of a kind. Those without luck have to play crummy, mismatched low cards and hope they catch something on the draw that just might produce a winning hand. Dave wanted to throw away all the cards he had been dealt, take his chances and draw a fresh hand. He gave up that notion and decided what he really wanted was simply to have a good horse, some cattle to run and a chunk of country where no man had ever set foot. That way he would never have to share the peace and quiet with anybody, and nobody would be counting on him for a goddamned thing.

Dave continued to stand outside the phone booth on a strip of black asphalt in the depressing grip of the night. Time lost definition. His thoughts flattened into a uniform gray like the night, like the shades of his frustrations, disappointments, resentments and his bitter unhappiness. He wiped away his tears, and his eyes—sunken and dark-rimmed—narrowed to poisonous black slits. Jaw muscles tightened and jumped. And then, with purpose, he marched into the nearby lounge, past the fifteen chromium selector levers of the cigarette machine and slammed a clenched fist against the polished grain of the wooden bar. He ordered a double Black Velvet. It was the kind of bar lacking in live music and nobody was playing the jukebox. There were no mirrors or reflective surfaces, no annoying clacking sounds of pool balls or the flash and ring of a pinball machine. A few solitary drinkers were lined up in the dark staring at their drinks and occasionally pushing fingers through the wet rings a drink will leave on wood. Dave fit right in with the purposeful drinkers. He was wearing his normal attire; blue jeans, a western shirt with pearl snaps, sleeves rolled to his elbows. The only item that set him apart was the cowboy hat tugged down low on his forehead. He rotated a toothpick, moving it from one side of his mouth to the other. He looked as if he had seen a lifetime of rodeos as he drank his whiskey, wincing with painful satisfaction, as if some bone inside him kept breaking and snapping back into place. He drank until the bar closed, and then he drove drunk on back roads, navigating through cavernous potholes; an owl flashed in and out of the tunneling headlights, a rabbit crossed the road and stood off to one side, eyes glowing red, and a gaunt coyote, like a wisp of gray smoke, appeared for an instant and was gone. The washboard road made Dave's teeth chatter, and he took swigs from the bottle making sure not to chip a tooth as his pickup hammered over the corduroy road.

Upon reaching the refuge of his trailer, Dave turned off the motor and sat in the silent darkness of his pickup truck. He took a quick inventory, like someone who had fallen might do upon regaining some semblance of consciousness. He was home in one piece. His brows were pinched down tight contemplating a crazy, inconsequential thought; if a person who felt compelled to jump from the railing of a bridge had a sense of relief, of contentment and satisfaction, upon hitting the water. After all, that was the climax, the ending bought and paid for with their life. As quickly as it had entered, Dave gave up that line of thought. His mouth and throat were dry and tainted. A headache was skewered from temple to temple. He clutched the neck of the bottle sitting on the seat beside him and drank to cleanse his mouth and throat; to cleanse his mind.

*****

Dave went inside and settled himself on the couch in his trailer. The voice he was so familiar with spoke once again. But this time the promise was not to have him at forty. This time the words were much more sinister and threatening. The bullying voice said *I hope I do not have to take one of your children.*

Dave groaned in agony, leaned forward and shook his head to be rid of the spell like a dog shaking water from its ears. It was of no use and he rolled off the couch and onto the floor. He cussed and he swore. He called God every vile name he could think of, spitting out words like sucked venom. He raged until he passed out and was dragged down into the black hole of oblivion.

When he awoke, Dave felt as though every organ in his body had been removed, and every drop of fluid had been drained from him. He was empty of life, exhausted, and did not possess the strength necessary to continue on. Yet he managed to feel around, find his bottle and pour a tall glass of Black Velvet. He drank it all. The alcohol calmed him and gave him the fortitude and the energy required to heave his body into an upright position. He sat for a long time, had another drink, got up off the floor and went to work with that hideous voice—he knew now it was Satan—ringing in his head. *I hope I do not have to take one of your children.*

Chapter Five

A haze of light touched eyelids. They fluttered to reveal a cloudy grayness marbled with pink and gold. Awareness tottered and faltered, tiptoed forward and Dave felt a delicate sensation of time, or the passage of time, and the brutality of his aching body lying on the coolness of the floor—hips and shoulders and head bearing the brunt of that pain—the sleeping bag was tugged haphazardly over his legs. A single friendless thought abruptly invaded Dave's mind; that the loss of a child is the most terrible of all nightmares for any father to have to try to endure. He questioned why his children were now suddenly being thrust into this mess, *his* mess. They had nothing to do with any of it. They were innocent victims. This was his fight; his fight alone. Dave was unsure of his opponent. Was it God, or was it Satan? Whichever deity was responsible needed to back off and leave his daughters the hell out of it.

Dave took another drink to steady himself, and it was then it hit him, hit him hard like an eight-pound maul swung into his gut. Working and living as he was in Apple Valley, he was worthless to his family. Why should he continue to live and thereby put his children in peril? They were better off with him dead; they would be safe and have his million dollar life insurance policy to spend. He was so damned tired, exhausted from lack of sleep, trying to measure up to his own expectations and humiliated by his insurmountable failures. He had brought shame and dishonor to himself and his family. He loathed his unquenchable craving for alcohol. He wished he was dead.

Dave had tried—on numerous occasions—had tried to quit drinking, but after a day or two of abstinence, delirium tremens seized him in its tightfisted grip. His body shivered and shook violently, until he feared his teeth would rattle out of his skull. He hallucinated: saw snakes that hissed and struck at him, lizards, spiders and rats. His heart raced until he imagined it would pound itself through his ribcage. He was confused and disoriented, mad and afraid. When he returned to consciousness his body was crammed into a corner of his trailer, cowering like a fearful child. He would not go through the DTs again. He could not.

For Dave there was no middle ground to consider. He certainly never wasted time contemplating himself as an old man; Peggy at his side, surrounded by the girls, all grown and mothers, his grandchildren by their sides, him a used up husk of a man lying in a hospital bed with oxygen fed to him from a pharmacy bottle, hospital gown wrapped around bony shoulders, chrome tray holding color-coded pills—take these—for Dave life would never ebb away like a lazy river bleeding off toward the sea. It was all coming down to one thing, guts. Did he have the guts to do this thing?

Dave, his thinking as flat and obstinate as a foot of fresh snow, devised a plan. It came to him over the span of days, or maybe it was weeks. It would be his last act of defiance against a God who had given him life; a God that Dave believed had abandoned him. Once Dave had reached that final decision, had accepted it in his mind as the right thing to do, he felt an enormous sense of relief. Gone were his imperfections and feelings of vulnerability. Gone were his weaknesses and sense of powerlessness. He retrieved the 12 gauge shotgun from where it was leaning against the cabinet by the door in his trailer, jacked the shell from the chamber, and the three in the magazine. The shells landed harmlessly on the couch; the ejecting mechanism made a bone-chilling grinding sound of finality.

Always one to diligently keep his gun clean—Dave cleaned it three or four times a year—and the gun had never let him down, never jammed, never rusted, never misfired. From a box of loose ammunition and supplies he picked out a discolored rag that was soft with oil soaked into it over the years, making it as limp as a wet dishrag. Dave took a small plastic bottle and squeezed more oil onto the cloth—some folks mistakenly put WD-40 on a gun, and though that makes the stock and barrel slick and shiny for a while, it soon evaporates and leaves behind a sticky residue—but Dave stuck to the tested and true gun oil, as he always had, to protect the weapon against rust. He told himself that the gun loved oil the way a cow loves green grass. He smiled and did not know why he had come up with such a far-fetched analogy or why he even cared about the gun. Soon it would all be over. His innocent family would be safe from danger, and well taken care of financially. For all Dave cared, God and Satan could fight over his miserable soul. He did not much care one way or the other which of the competing forces, good or evil, might win the battle.

Dave had made himself a solid promise; he would have one last drink, then walk out on the desert, put the end of the shotgun barrel inside his mouth and pull the trigger. Ending it would be as simple as that. He had even tested the procedure to make sure he could reach the trigger and had been left with the sweetly sour, and yet not totally disagreeable taste of Hoppe's gun oil on his lips. But Dave, in his moment of supreme crisis, had a need that superseded even the taking of his life. He had to make sure his crew was positioning the trusses on his warehouse correctly, and maintaining the strict schedule for completion by the end of July. When he was satisfied all was in order, he would return to his trailer, have that drink, take that walk, and end his life.

Dave got in his pickup truck and drove toward his warehouse jobsite. On the way he passed a trailer where damp clothes flapped on a line surrounded by a moat of abandoned junk: milk crates full of automobile parts, trailers, rusting oil barrels and a fiberglass boat with a hole punched through the bow. A little girl was playing on a cheap swing set. She swung back and forth; her feet extending forward, pumping, and her ponytail flying out behind her. A small white dog sat on its haunches watching.

The little girl reminded Dave of his daughters back home in Oregon. But they were teenagers now, nearly grown. This time of the year they would be getting their steers ready for the 4-H fair; washing and brushing and teaching the animals to lead with a halter. He wished he could be there to help them. He missed them so much he cried. After the tears he thought about the Powell Butte ranch and the enjoyable acts: moving cows from one pasture to another, driving tractor under the burning summer sun, building fences, catching calves and putting tags in their ears, feeding, momma cows bawling for their calves and calves bawling for their mommas at weaning time. He thought about some simple acts he suddenly missed; opening a head-gate and sending a charge of water down a ditch, and he missed the simple act of shoving leather gloves into the gullet of his saddle as the day warmed. He grinned with tight lips at his sharp stab of nostalgia.

When Dave turned off the road and into the jobsite he saw the last of the trusses being lifted by a crane and placed on the top of the warehouse. He got out of his pickup and squinted into the bright sunlight undulating through haze, or smog, or clouds stretched thin like taffy. The men were busy working. All was taken care of. All was right with this one small corner of the world.

For a long moment Dave remained rooted to one spot, his attention drawn to a lone vulture—soaring, circling, feathered wingtips flaring to touch the thermal updraft it was surfing—

lifting ever higher and becoming more distant, a tiny speck of dark in the tall void of blue sky. Dave turned away and had almost reached his pickup when a white Toyota flatbed truck wheeled through in a hurried rush, coming to an abrupt stop a few steps away from Dave. A cloud of powdery dust blew through, engulfed the pickup for an instant and rushed past. There was a steel rack attached to the flatbed, extending above the cab; ladders tied on top gave the appearance of a typical painter's rig.

When two men exited—white coveralls splattered with a muted rainbow of colors—they confirmed they were indeed painters. Both men were big and overweight. The driver, a thin sheen of sweat on his flushed face, stepped forward and withdrew a red rag from a hip pocket and proceeded to mop sweat from his brow.

"I imagine you fellows are here to bid the job," said Dave. He was apathetic and did not care if these men bid the job. He just wanted to get rid of them as quickly as possible and go kill himself.

"We're not here to bid your job, mister," said the driver.

Then the driver proceeded to introduce himself and his partner—Ed Shelton and Mike Delahanty—but neither man made any effort to shake Dave's hand, or ask his name. Ed took a step closer and again Dave noted the size of the man and he questioned, *If they aren't here to bid the job, what the hell are they here for?* Ed, with a hardened gaze that never wavered, was looking Dave square in the eyes. Dave wanted to turn away, but did not.

Somewhere nearby a Caterpillar—wrenched and welded together by a beer-guzzling mechanic—was clearing a pad for yet another warehouse. The growl of the diesel engine increased a few decibels, steel tracks churned gray sand, black smoke puffed from the smokestack into the azure sky. The sharp blade ripped, tore, and pushed a tall Joshua tree—the tree named by Mormon settlers after the biblical leader, Joshua. The tree reminded them of their hero, raising outstretched arms toward the heavens—and for a brief moment the roots held tight as the gnarled top of the tree drew errant circles in the sky. The trunk began to lean slowly, bending to one side like the mast of a sailing ship on a storm-tossed sea. Reluctantly the tree toppled, landing with a resistive and feeble thud. The blade pushed away the soft, sullen earth that had remained hidden for millenniums, but was now being exposed to the unflinching sun. Soil lay curled and cracked. Overhead a flock of gulls—so far from the ocean their appearance seemed ludicrous—wheeled across the desert sky, calling caustically, and impatiently waiting for the opportunity to swoop down and devour any worms, bugs or insects; if indeed there were any for them to eat.

Ed Shelton had not shaved that morning, had not combed his hair or brushed his teeth, and probably had not showered either. He addressed Dave and posed a single question. "Do you know Jesus Christ?"

"What?" Dave threw up his hands and a sudden cloudburst of tears stung his eyes. He took an involuntary step backward and blindly felt for the door handle of his pickup truck. He opened the door and sat heavily on the seat, feet dangling, hands held limply across his lap. Dave, in a flurry of blistering words, showed his annoyance and aggravation, hissing, "Don't you son of a bitches show up at my jobsite talking to me about Jesus Christ. I've got more troubles than anyone can imagine. I've got more trouble than any man on the face of this goddamned earth."

"That's why we're here," said Ed. "To pray for you." His voice was very calm and controlled, almost soothing. Then that giant of a man dressed in the simple white garb of a painter lowered himself onto his knees in front of Dave. He folded his hands above his massive girth and began to pray.

"Dear Lord God, I was getting ready for work and You spoke to me and said there was a man in trouble and I had to find him. I tried to send Mike to the job, but he said he was coming with me. We drove all the way up from San Bernardino. You directed which roads

to take, down the freeway, back along the service road, then turn onto Bear Creek Road and finally to where we are now. When we arrived and met this man from that very moment I knew this was the man You had sent us to find, and to pray for."

Dave felt extremely self-conscious, glanced over his left shoulder and saw his crew—they were supposed to be rolling rafters—had stopped working and the men were now gawking over the side of the building at the drama that was transpiring on the ground. What could Dave do? He certainly could not interrupt this burly man on his knees, tell him to stop praying, to get up and leave.

"Jesus Christ, our Lord savior, I ask that You come to this man in his hour of great desperation and that You light his way and bring him peace. I ask that You relieve him from his suffering, that You lift the tremendous weight of his many burdens and worries. In the name of Jesus Christ, please accept this man into your heavenly folds. Amen."

With effort, Ed Shelton got to his feet. He clasped one of Dave's hands in both of his beefy hands and said, "We will pray for you." And then Ed Shelton and Mike Delahanty departed in their flatbed truck with ladders tied on top of the metal rack. The men on the roof of the warehouse returned to their work. Dave continued to sit with his legs dangling down out of the truck. He could not move and he was crying and trying to make some semblance of what had just transpired. Who the hell were those men dressed in the simple garb of painters? They had obviously been directed to the jobsite. Who sent them? Had it really been God who sent them? They sure as hell did not look like angels. Dave smiled at such a thought, and his troubles no longer seemed as oppressive as they once had. *We will pray for you.* Dave was not sure what he felt, perhaps it was the tinniest flicker of ... hope.

*****

Dave returned to his trailer and poured himself that drink, just as he promised he would do, filling the glass to the brim with Black Velvet. He never took so much as a sip. Instead he sat on the couch and stared ahead at the calendar tacked to the cupboard door. The Fourth of July had come and gone. More dates in July were marked through with a big red X than were unmarked. His 41st birthday was approaching in only a few short days.

I will have you at forty.
I hope I don't have to take one of your children.

*****

One moment Dave was sitting in the 1977 Terry Trailer with the last vestige of the hot desert sun slanting through the windows, and the next he awoke and it was the darkest of nights. Yet he knew where he was, walking out across the 101 Flat, a remote spot between Prineville and Dayville in far away Eastern Oregon; a place where Dave often herded sheep when he was a boy. This was not a vision, or a hallucination, or some strange figment of Dave's imagination. He could tell with each of his five senses that somehow his body had been miraculously transported a thousand miles to the 101 Flat. Off to his immediate right was Antone Road. To the left, miles away, was the deep canyon carved by the John Day River.

Ahead, a glowing orb of tender light the color of pale jade became faintly visible; a smoky, diffused light that grew in intensity. It drew Dave forward—ever closer—until he was near enough to witness the vague image of a man standing in the center of that incredible shaft of brightness. His image became stronger and took on definition and form. His hair was long— the delicate shade of polished oak—falling to his shoulders and beyond. The man was as thin as a tree branch, and his skin as white and lucent as the open palm of a candle filled with a pool of melted wax. His facial features were long and narrow, almost skeletal, with a defined sharpness to the structure of his bones. But it was the eyes that made the face; oval and outrageously beautiful. Eyes that reached out in a gentle and radiantly happy embrace; eyes soothing, calming, and yet so powerful and nourishing and all encompassing they diminished anything of this earth. The eyes were love in its purest form; an incredible love not confined by limits, or borders, or any recognized form of restraint. Was the pigmentation of those eyes blue, green, brown, or a combination of colors? Color ceased to exist. All that remained was that incredible sense of love radiating from within those eyes. They encircled all things in a cleansing wash of passion and power. Dave's tensions, despair, misery, anguish and hopelessness melted away to nothingness.

Dave had squandered his life in search of absolute love; had tried to find it in marriage, family, business, money, possessions, power and control. And he had tried to find it in his abuse of alcohol. But now, as he stood within the orb of this light, this stranger who Dave knew well—but had spent his life rejecting—had finally given him the love he needed to sustain him. Dave basked in the happiness and warmth of that astonishing love. This then was the missing piece, and with this missing piece a perfect portrait had been formed.

"Jesus," said Dave in recognition and greeting. The shining sphere of radiance began moving forward, not walking, but floating. Dave followed. He was not walking either, he too was floating. They moved in unison—Jesus and Dave—like a pair of doves at nightfall flying wingtip to wingtip. Dave accepted the notion that he was now in the presence of Jesus. They reached a point where the old road crossed over and dropped into Mountain Creek. Dave felt compelled to ask a question. "Where is the road that used to be here?"

"I don't know anything about that," said Jesus. The words came forth soft and poignant, each word carrying weight and significance, and yet those words were as subtle and distinct as the tapping of a stiff feather on the stretched skin of a drum. *I don't know anything about that.*

They continued following Mountain Creek, moving with ease, without effort. Distance and time had no relevance. The countryside was breathtakingly beautiful, as is seldom seen—only after an incredibly wet spring when the days grow long and warm—with flowers blooming and the grass green and lush and knee high. Dave thought how the band of sheep his family once owned would have loved to graze on grass this verdant and nutritious.

Upon reaching the bottom of the draw, where Mountain Creek makes a quick zag and bleeds off into another draw, Jesus led the way up and over a series of ridges. The distance, as measured on a map, was probably greater than ten miles and yet it was nothing. As they moved, Jesus kept His steadfast gaze on Dave. There was such kindness in His eyes. Dave glided blissfully in the all-encompassing cloud of God's love.

At the summit of the fourth ridge Jesus stopped. A warm night wind sighed along the crest and the countryside was spread out below them, bathed in the light of the Heavenly Being. From this vantage the land sloped gently, dropping onto flats and into swales and hidden valleys all flowing gently down to join with the John Day River drainage. The only way anyone ever saw this country was on horseback; there were no roads. Dave had spent many summers during his growing-up-years on the back of his horse watching over the sheep as they ranged across this remote landscape.

Dave knew that below the ridge, at a point where a freshwater spring issued from the rocky hillside, was Jerry's cabin—named for the old homesteader who first settled on the property and claimed a desert entry to 320 acres of land. The timber to make the cabin had been felled with an axe and crosscut saw and the logs snaked to the building site with a team of work horses. Dave and the herder, Mike Corley, had spent many a night in the cabin. Dave looked now, assuming he would see the cabin as well as the tree where, when he came in from a day of riding, he always hung his saddle and blanket on a dead branch so the horse's sweat could dry in the cool night air. But the familiar landmark was gone. It was as though Jerry's cabin had never existed. But the tree was where it should be; just as it had always been, with the sawed off limb.

"Where is the cabin that used to be there?" asked Dave.

And Jesus replied, *I don't know about that.*

Dave wanted to shout, "But you are Jesus. You should know what happened to Jerry's cabin. What happened to it?" Dave could never bring himself to utter those words. His attention was drawn away to a band of sheep spread across the hillside grazing. These sheep were not like the sheep he remembered; a dingy gray stain languidly shifting like seaweed swilling with the currents. These sheep were shockingly white, as white and unblemished as new fallen snow. Again Dave turned to Jesus and this time asked in his astonishment, "How do you keep the sheep so white?"

I do not know them any other way, replied Jesus.

Dave shrugged his shoulders and meekly replied, "Well, okay." Uttering those two words seemed to require all of Dave's breath and he waited until he thought he could speak once more and asked, "How do you keep the grass so green?"

And Jesus replied, *Someday you will know.*

Again Dave shrugged, a helpless gesture, and he muttered, "Okay." And he let it go at that. When he looked back at the hillside, where the sheep had been, he saw all the animals of the world had been gathered together and were resting peacefully. There were lions and tigers, giraffes and grizzly bears, gazelles, elk, buffalo and rabbits. It was amazing and so very difficult for Dave to take all of what he was seeing into his mind and process it as factual. He felt lightheaded and found it difficult to breathe. He tried to calm his emotions. He surveyed the multitude of animals that all seemed so docile and serene. This sight certainly defied any reasonable explanation. All Dave could do was to accept that the animals were there. He never thought to ask Jesus why.

Jesus started down off the ridge, following the approximate route they had traveled, and as they moved through the tall grasses, Dave kept thinking he was wasting precious time, that he needed to ask Jesus more questions. Why had he been given so many troubles to endure? How could he earn back the respect he lost with the collapse of his construction company? How could he reclaim his family? But more than anything he wanted to admit to Jesus he was a sinner, an alcoholic, and he was powerless to stop drinking. He wanted to ask Jesus for His help in facing his personal demon. He wanted to ask for forgiveness.

When they reached Mountain Creek, Dave instinctively knew their trails would soon part; he would go one way, and Jesus would go another. He stopped and Jesus stopped. Dave blurted his question, "Do you remember when I used to...."

Jesus interrupted. He said, *I don't remember*.

Those words, *I don't remember*, swept over Dave like a cresting wave that washed away everything he had held inside for so long. He wept, and he could not stop weeping. The aura surrounding Jesus began to move away. Dave wanted to shout, "Stay with me!" But he only sensed joy. He had walked with Jesus. Jesus had forgiven him his sins. *I don't remember.* Dave no longer felt anger and bitterness. He no longer felt guilt, regret, shame. He did not hate himself for his weaknesses. *I don't remember.* Absolution.

*****

Dave awoke lying on the couch in the Terry Trailer with his head pressed into the vinyl cushion. Hours had passed. The room was pitch black and yet Dave instinctively could sense where he was—could feel the damp cushion in his face wet from his tears—and he did not want to be there. He wanted to go back once again to the 101 Flat and walk with Jesus. He wanted to feast on the astonishing love he had felt. He wanted more, wanted to submerse himself and feel the joyous buoyancy of God's love.

Dave could not return to 101 Flat. He could not walk in unison with Jesus. He sobbed, "No," and it came out guttural, more like a feeble groan than an actual word. He tried to push his face away from the wet cushion. He rolled to one side and fell off the narrow couch and onto the floor. He brought his knees up to his chest. He was still sobbing and he cried out in anguish and despair, "Jesus."

Dave remained on the floor, the cool of early morning came creeping in, and still he did not move. He was trapped in his wondrous experience when he had basked in the all-powerful and encompassing embrace of God's love. God was strong. Dave was pitifully weak. Even now his body craved alcohol. Or was Satan speaking and telling him he needed that drink? He wanted to hoist himself off the floor, take that glass of Black Velvet on the counter where he had set it—it was to be his last drink—and take a long, satisfying gulp of whiskey. He knew alcohol was at the root of his many problems and he called out in misery, "God, give me strength. I will live for you if you make me a strong man." And as soon as he uttered those words the craving went away and once more Dave was surrounded by the tender sea of God's love. He slept right there on the floor.

Chapter Six

Dave did not feel as though he could share with anyone his wondrous experience of having walked with Jesus. He knew if he tried to explain, mere words would fail him, fail miserably. It was even more likely people would disbelieve him, claim he had lost his mind, or try to explain his vision away as a vivid hallucination caused by alcohol. Dave realized, at least for the time being, he had to keep his encounter with Jesus strictly to himself.

Dave still craved alcohol. Every molecule of his body craved alcohol, and though he did give in to his demon, he made a conscious effort to drink less. When overcome with the compulsion for another drink, he often asked God for strength, and sometimes that did work; for a while it worked.

One Sunday morning, Dave awoke hearing the cooing of mourning doves and he remembered Sunday mornings at home, the family getting ready to go to church. Dave had an impulsive desire to go to church. He had noticed the Pentecostal

Church in Apple Valley and he got up, got dressed and drove there. By the time he arrived at the church the service was over and people were sitting on metal folding chairs listening to a woman in the Sunday School Class talk about the importance of forgiveness in our lives. There were maybe a hundred people gathered, mostly young couples, some with children. Dave took a seat in the back row. The lady speaker interrupted her lesson to acknowledge Dave's presence and to thank him for coming.

Dave was embarrassed at the attention and was sure he would not know anyone in the church, but as he gazed out over the backs of the congregation, there in the third row from the front, was a burly-shouldered man and Dave immediately recognized him as Ed Shelton, one of the painters who had come to pray for him. He was not an angel after all like Dave had come to believe. He was a living, breathing human being and that revelation startled Dave.

Ed turned and looked over his shoulder, and when he saw Dave he stood and began making his way to the back of the room. He moved slowly, more of a waddle than walk, like an old bear coming out of hibernation. His wife, a small woman in a loose-fitting dress, was at his side.

Upon reaching Dave, Ed said, "I'm glad to see you here." He grabbed Dave roughly, pulled him to his feet and hugged him. Ed went on to explain, "We're not members of this church. We usually go to church in San Bernardino. We thought it would be a nice day for a drive. That's why we're here."

Dave did not know what to say, what he should say to the man who had prayed for him and helped save his life. Dave did not want to cry. He tried not to cry. But he did cry and he told Ed, "Thank you." With those words spoken he turned and hurried away.

*****

Summer was coming to an end and Dave had not confided his godly vision to anyone. He called Peggy at least once a week, and they talked about normal things; business dealings, the continuing battle with the IRS, the kids and the animals and sometimes a bit of lighthearted gossip from the Powell Butte neighborhood. Dave talked about the hot weather, the constant wind that blew the dust around, how the building was going, and if he picked up a new project he shared the details of what was involved.

Dave felt, by withholding something as vitally important as his experience of walking with Jesus from his wife, that a small division between them now existed. He feared, in time, that division would be like a tiny crack in a rock that eventually splits the rock apart. Dave wanted to tell Peggy, but how was he ever going to stand in a phone booth in the desert and relate such a thing.

Peggy felt something was different, but she could never put her finger on exactly what that something might be. It just seemed as though Dave was more ... maybe he seemed more content—not happy—just more at ease and calm. She never asked questions. She never pressed him. If Dave had something to tell her, he would tell her in due time. That was how Peggy handled any conflict. Conflict was like a slow dance to Peggy and she always allowed Dave to lead that dance.

It took all of the courage Dave could muster, and a lot of prayers, for him to place a call to Peggy and ask if she would meet him. He said he figured Redding would be about equal distance. He had made reservations at the Hilltop Motel for the coming Friday and Saturday nights. He gave Peggy the address and told her how to get there. Then he mentioned the motel had a swimming pool.

"This is unexpected," said Peggy. She was not quite sure what to make of Dave's proposed weekend rendezvous. The details of making arrangements for someone to watch her daughters, and the long drive to Redding, momentarily distracted her. She had nothing to say for a moment.

"Just the two of us," said Dave encouragingly. "Maybe we can try to get to know each other all over again."

"Okay," said Peggy. The word hung open-ended until she added, "See you Friday."

Dave did not want his wife to hang up, to end their conversation. He added, "I need to talk to you about something."

"What?" asked Peggy as her mind raced with wild possibilities: Was Dave going to tell her about a new construction project on the horizon? Was Dave going to surprise her by announcing he was moving the family to Guatemala or Mexico City? It could be anything, and the anything part was what concerned Peggy the most.

"We can talk about it when I see you," said Dave. "Give the girls a hug for me. I love you."

"I love you, too," Peggy added before she hung up the receiver.

*****

Dave and Peggy arrived at the Hilltop Motel at nearly the same time. What amazed Peggy about their reunion was that Dave appeared to be an entirely different man. His demeanor was almost timid and the tensions and worries he had carried in the knit of his brow and the set of his jaw were no longer there. He was relaxed and seemed more like the man he was in his younger years, a man who knew he was in charge without demanding dominance.

It was not until the following day, while they were floating in the motel swimming pool—on air mattresses Peggy had thought to bring along, when Dave told her the motel had a swimming pool—when Dave finally began to reveal more. He spoke with neither reluctance nor eagerness; his journey of words began like a mountain climber ascending a tall peak, taking one methodical step after another.

Dave started by saying, "I've got something I need to share." He began with going to the warehouse jobsite and the sudden appearance of Ed Shelton and Mike Delahanty. "I was checking to make sure the men were rolling out the trusses on the warehouse when this pickup came racing in and two big men, dressed in painters' coveralls, climbed out...."

A bird, Dave thought it might be a Grosbeak because of the lively red, yellow and white feathers, landed on the chain link fence surrounding the pool, sang a series of lyrical notes and flew away. Overhead, the trail of a passing jet, needle-sharp on one end and the other barely distinguishable from the powder blue of the sky, moved stealthily, soundlessly south. Even though it felt to Dave like his blood had turned to gas and was now whistling through his arteries and veins, he described in lurid details the painters praying for him, and then his vision of the brilliant orb of light he had witnessed on the 101 Flat, of seeing Jesus in that light, but when he tried to explain how he felt—so inferior in the presence of Jesus—he faltered and tearfully mumbled he was surrounded by a sensation of love, a love he had never before experienced in his life.

All through the telling—his conversations with Jesus, the white sheep on the hillside, all the animals of the world existing in harmony and on to the final question he posed to Jesus and His answer, *I don't remember*—he cried, his voice cracked and broke with emotion. Every once in a while a wayward puff of wind passing over the pool lifted the hairs on Dave's forearms, causing his fingers to twitch.

The story moved at its own languid pace—a startling story for Peggy to hear—and when it concluded, the spoken words that had been expressed with so much heartfelt and sincere emotion, lay orphaned between them. Peggy broke the silence. She told Dave she admired his courage for telling her. And she told him she had prayed and prayed for just such a moment as this.

In baring his soul—exposing himself to doubt and scorn like a prizefighter who voluntarily enters the ring with his arms tied behind his back and is content to absorb any punishment his opponent might inflict—Dave was left feeling completely beaten and drained. It had taken every ounce of nerve he could muster to confide his secret. And now he had completed what he needed to accomplish and was pleased with Peggy's response.

For Peggy, there were two sides for her to consider. Yes, her prayers had been answered, a miracle had occurred and Dave had welcomed the Lord into his life, but she had to question what effect this *new Dave* might have on her life, and the lives of their daughters. She knew how to handle the brash, belligerent, bull-headed, alcoholic Dave. The Dave who, if he came up against an obstruction, used anger to bulldoze his way through; and if that failed, he obliterated the barrier with determination and rage. The new personality Dave now exhibited was nothing like the old Dave. No longer did the predictability of alcohol fuel Dave's energy and elevate his dominant personality to an unstoppable presence.

Peggy now felt the tension she was holding in her back and neck muscles, and the beginnings of a headache forming between her temples. The sun lingered over the pool, causing Peggy to shiver in its light. She crossed her arms and closed her eyes against that brazen sun. She let out a pent up breath, so soft Dave never heard it, but to Peggy it sounded like a moan of resignation.

After she had returned home, Peggy tried to put everything she had been exposed to into some sort of perspective. She loved Dave, she knew that. She replayed what he had said to her in the swimming pool in Redding—seeing Dave's anguish, hearing his words, running it all back and forth—and she still did not know what to think. The new Dave alarmed her. She did not know what to expect; what was coming next. She tried to prepare herself for the unknown, but that was impossible. Peggy was in a quandary, unsure how she was supposed to react to Dave and his emerging personality.

*****

Now more than ever Dave felt the need to be with Peggy and the girls. He made a unilateral decision to finish his work in Apple Valley and move home to Central Oregon. But even thinking about buttoning up his projects in Southern California and heading home caused Dave a tremendous amount of anguish. So much so that he fell back to old habits and once again resorted to alcohol to give him energy and nerve. Then when he did give in to alcohol, he loathed his weakness. He called on God—*give me strength*.

Dave's moods varied wildly; from one moment thinking he could conquer the world and reach the pinnacle of financial success where he had once stood, to seeing himself as a contemptible excuse for a human being and a failure. His frame of mind depended on whether he was drunk or sober. Most of the time his disposition was somewhere between the two divergent extremes: he was sullen, withdrawn, easily agitated and quick to flash his unruly temper.

The morning arrived when the ultimate decision had to be made. Would Dave stay in Apple Valley or would he return home to his family in Central Oregon? He wavered, knowing if he stuck to his plan he would be accountable to Peggy and his daughters. They would know if he was drinking. In addition to their scrutiny and the judgment they would pass, Dave had to face his friends. He was not sure he possessed the courage to do that—to admit he was an alcoholic. He prayed and asked for God's guidance.

There was no clear-cut resolution, no voice telling Dave what he should do. Finally he hauled himself up off the couch where he had been lying, threw the sleeping bag in a pile on the floor and went outside and pushed the stinger into place on the hitch and attached the tongue of his trailer to the chrome ball. He opened the door of his pickup truck and climbed behind the wheel. He tapped the gas feed a time or two and the old motor turned over, coughed a couple times and sprang to life. Sunshine was glinting on the windshield dust and Dave's gut, in need of alcohol, grumbled and rolled. *God give me strength*.

Dave resolutely started the journey north. How many times did he pull over at a wide spot to either pray, or sneak a drink from his bottle of courage? So many times he lost count. About the same number of times he came to a crossroads, and it took all his willpower not to veer away from his intended route and lose himself in a place where nobody would know him, where he would not be accountable or forced to live up to anyone's expectations. A place where he could drink until drinking killed him.

Every mile Dave traveled he thought, "Will I be accepted?" That lonely possibility of rejection played heavily on his mind and filled him with doubt. Would Peggy and the girls welcome him with open arms? He knew in his heart they would. But they had been forced to fend for themselves for a long time; had their own routines and their own lives. Dave would have to adjust and fit in. He did not know if he could be subservient to their needs. And what about his friends—drinking buddies really—how would they react if he was not drinking with them? Alcohol was their shared existence. It was what they had in common, a mutual validation, and in most instances it was all they had in common. Take away the presence of alcohol and what was left? Dave doubted the depth of his resolve— he doubted himself—and foresaw an easy slide back into his former habits.

Dave arrived home and, of course, Peggy and the girls did welcome him with open arms. When Dave informed his friends that he no longer drank alcohol, they seemed to respect his choice and his resolve. They claimed it was for the best, and rarely drank in his presence. None of them wanted to be the party responsible for tempting Dave and causing him to fall off his self-imposed wagon. Life swirled in a tight, familiar spiral of good and not so good; just life.

Dave wanted to throw himself into work, but the building recession in Central Oregon continued, and the small amount of construction that remained invariably went to the few established companies that had somehow managed to survive. Dave bid every job he could find and even low-balled his bids to try and re-establish his construction company. His bids were consistently rejected. Dave became discouraged and depressed. He had never been the type of man who could do nothing. He had to have a host of projects on the horizon to occupy his mind and burn away his energy. Dave began escaping, going off alone; driving the back roads in his pickup truck or riding a horse across the sagebrush and juniper studded hills around Powell Butte.

Peggy took a job as the assistant to the manager of the Crook County Fairgrounds. At the end of each day she came home to find Dave even more sullen and discouraged. She tried to cheer him, telling him to be patient; that the economy would eventually rebound. For the most part, Peggy and the girls struggled to stay out of Dave's way and continue on with the lives they had been living.

One of the girls asked Peggy, "What's up with Dad?" Peggy defended Dave, saying they were living through difficult times. "He's so different," said the daughter. "I liked him better when he swore and was angry all the time."

*****

Dave had quit drinking while he was still living in Apple Valley and had endured the terrible effects of delirium tremens; being pushed to the brink of what he could endure physically and mentally. He re-emerged on the far side because of his will to live, and his desire to be reunited with his family. Then he stumbled, fell back to his old ways, and after coming home, he occasionally still drank. Mostly he did not feed the demon inside his body that was stimulated by alcohol. He worked hard at staying sober and was consumed by shame when he faltered and drank.

The changes in Dave's personality were obvious; he was no longer brash and angry and quick to curse. Now he never uttered the Lord's name in vain. For the most part he controlled his temper and his anger seldom flared and when it did he was quick to apologize. But not all the changes were good. Before he had been casual about going to church and now he was fanatical that the family was together on Sunday morning and that they attend church as a family. Rarely did Dave show any sense of humor. He was very judgmental and rigid. He was unable to relax and it seemed that nobody could ever do anything the way Dave wanted it done; not his daughters and certainly not

Peggy. Peggy went out of her way to do little things that in the past had pleased Dave. Now he refused to notice if there were candles lit on the dinner table, berry cobbler for dessert, a chocolate kiss on his pillow. Dave was too self-absorbed, and so fearful of backsliding, that he refused to allow himself even the slightest indulgence or pleasure. His life seemed to be one of fear and constant denial.

*****

It was well past time for Dave to share with his daughters the story of his conversation with Jesus and to tell of his battle with the demon he was fighting every waking hour of his existence. He put off the family talk several times—one of the girls was gone to spend the night with a friend, or there was a show on television one of them had her heart set on seeing—but finally Dave made up his mind. He would call everyone together right after dinner, and then he put that off until it was almost the girls' bedtime.

Dave prepared for the event by turning off most of the lights in the spacious living room and building a fire in the wood stove. Light from the cheery flames showed through the glass doors and danced around the room. He called the girls by name and they came and curled up on chairs and couches, their feet tucked under them. Outside, the ever-present Powell Butte wind made the tree branches rattle and scrape dryly against the side of the house. As the girls waited for their father to talk, they eagerly searched Dave's face for any clue that might reveal why they were having this family meeting. This, they knew, was something out of the ordinary, and maybe even something stupendous might be coming that would affect them personally. They were afraid of what their father might reveal.

Dave cleared his throat once, twice. He paced. He stopped and in a very controlled voice, yet a voice laced with emotion, he said, "I have been on a journey, a very difficult journey. I want to be honest with you. I don't know if I can ever come back from this journey. With every ounce of strength I possess, I'm going to try to make this journey."

Peggy came into the room and took a seat. She remained aloof, distant from Dave and their daughters.

How was Dave going to explain that he was facing an adversary so formidable that his own strength was nothing in comparison? How could he tell his daughters that boldness and determination counted for almost nothing and that victory could only be measured by his survival? His willpower momentarily faltered, but only for a brief moment. He took a deep breath, filled his lungs and expelled the air with a rush. What choice did he have? He had to continue what he had started. It was one more step of his journey. A big step to be sure, but just one step. His daughters needed to know the demon their father was fighting. If he allowed the demon of alcohol to win, it would kill him and probably sooner than later. In their own lives his daughters needed to know this. They needed to know they too carried the gene of alcoholism. They alone would have to make decisions on what path they chose to follow and which attributes they would look for in a man to marry. But more than anything, Dave felt compelled to be truthful and honest. And if his daughters turned against him and hated him for his weakness, then that was the chance he had to be willing to take.

Dave's throat swelled and his airway constricted to an agonizing point. He was uncomfortable and embarrassed and not at all sure he could squeeze enough air over his vocal cords to elicit sound. He gathered himself—the way a horse will gather itself before plunging into a river or leaping a wide ditch—and he paced.

The girls were looking at their father, their eyes wide and questioning. He had their undivided and rapt attention. Never before had their father admitted to any chink in his armor, and now he was confessing that he was not invincible, that he was on a personal journey and did not know if he could return from this journey. He had gone away once before, running off to Apple Valley, and except for periodic visits he was gone from their lives. Was he saying he was abandoning them once again?

Light waned as the fire collapsed in on itself. Ash and embers ignited fresh wood, throwing off a fine mist of sparks and a steady orange light which followed Dave as he now moved in front of a bank of tall windows. A dark sky, twinkling starlight and a thin, crescent slice of moon were visible draped above the brooding outline of the distant mountains.

"I am fighting to save my soul, and my life," said Dave. "I have a terrible demon inside me. That demon is alcohol. I am an alcoholic. I desire whiskey the way a thirsty man craves water. This addiction I have is bigger than me. It makes me do things I don't want to do.

"I have a story to tell you, a story you need to hear," said Dave, and the words he spoke were weighted with the gravity of his self-loathing, regret, and grief; with his lament that he could not have been a stronger man. He told about the snakes that hissed in his face and vultures that circled waiting for him to die. Again he confessed his weakness for the alcohol that had kept him afloat. Dave thought it had been difficult talking to Peggy in the motel swimming pool, but that was a breeze compared to the faces of his four daughters and their eyes that filled with tears, tears that wetted their cheeks and made their pink skin glisten.

Dave had always viewed himself as the rock of the family. As his story unfolded the solidness of that rock cracked and crumbled into a heap of worthless dust. He was a failure, a broken down detestable excuse of a man. If his daughters condemned him for his imperfections, so be it—he sure as hell was guilty and deserved whatever came his way—but he did not want them to view his faults as their faults. He hated, truly hated himself, for having to put his children through this ordeal. Out in the darkness of the night Satan was laughing with delight.

The story made a sharp turn when Dave told about the two painters finding him and praying for him. He explained how he had been reborn in God's image and his vision of walking with Jesus on the 101 Flat. He described in intimate detail the way Jesus radiated light and love and how he felt saturated with that unblemished love. He stated each of the questions he had asked Jesus and the responses Jesus had given in return. He went on to disclose that because of this experience, he was now a changed man.

"I am on a journey," sobbed Dave once again. "I am going to fight with all the strength I possess to become a better man."

And then a miracle occurred. His oldest daughter, Marlece, stood up first, and the others quickly followed—Jenay, Tawnya and Shauna. They rushed to their father and embraced him. Dave's strength failed—his legs could no longer sustain his weight—and he slowly sank to his knees. Peggy joined them and they cried together, not tears of sorrow or despair, but tears of incredible joy.

"I don't know if I can make this journey," sobbed Dave.

"Yes, you can, Dad," said one of the girls.

"We are in this journey together," said another.

Peggy offered, "And God is with us on this journey."

Dave heard Satan groan in the distance and he cried all the harder, until he had no more tears to shed and then it was finally over.

Chapter Seven

The sun, hot and dry, chased the road dust into the truck and muddied Dave's throat to the point he told himself, "Damn I need a drink." But his misery of having had to face his daughters and admit he was an alcoholic was too fresh in his mind. Dave would not allow himself the indulgence of even a single drink, even though he knew there was at least one bottle under the seat and probably a couple more in the tool chest in the bed of his truck. His muscles quivered in anticipation and for a perilous moment Dave's blood ran thin through his arteries and heart. He felt worn out and used up. Wind whorled across his scalp and his thinning hair looked brittle and gray. But he did not give in—not that day—his weakness did not win.

Upon returning home from his drive, Dave found a message on the answering machine. A neighbor wanted to build a garage. He asked Dave to bid the job. That news lifted Dave's spirits immeasurably. He was proud he had not given in to temptation. Finally something with potential seemed poised on the horizon and he decided it was a fine day after all.

*****

Word made the rounds that Dave Franke had experienced a godly vision. He was asked to give testimony at the Powell Butte Church, but quickly declined. The reason he gave was that the experience was still too fresh, and in the telling he feared he would become overly emotional. Dave knew the real reason was because he did not want to stand in front of his peers and admit he was an alcoholic; and besides, he still doubted himself, his resolve not to revert and give in to his temptations. He was afraid his demon would return, return with a vengeance and that the alcohol would win and the devil would claim his soul. That was Dave's biggest fear. He did not want Satan to win.

What Dave found was that without a drink to prop him up, he was listless and his life lacked purpose and direction. He seemed to have lost his edge. Rather than being energetic and boisterous as he had been in his heyday, he was now withdrawn and unsure of himself when it came to making decisions. Alcohol had given him all those things his normal personality lacked. Alcohol buoyed his spirits, gave him confidence, made him believe in himself, provided unlimited energy and powered his ambitions. Without alcohol he felt he was less of a man.

Dave found it hard to concentrate on anything and at night he tossed and turned, rolling things over in his mind and listening to the house complain in the wind. Every sound seemed amplified and discontent, as if individual boards were protesting the tight framework of the house. Sometimes Dave left Peggy sleeping on her side of the bed and he got up and paced, walking through the house in his stocking feet, searching for what he lacked. He never conceded to the indulgence that would make him whole, but leave him broken and grief-stricken in its wake. He often stopped in front of the cabinet that once was home to his alcohol. It depressed Dave that he could not even keep a bottle around for company, but he was aware that a bottle was temptation. He could not give in to temptation and that fact made him crave alcohol all the more.

One night Dave lay in bed listening to the pounding of his heart in his ears. He turned his head and the noise deepened as blood throbbed in his skull; the sounds of his ragged breathing scared him even more and he was afraid his heart would stop beating; that he would stop breathing. He got up, wrapped a blanket around his shoulders and went out into the cold night and stood, watching his breath appear in a cloud of freezing condensation. He became aware of a strange scratching sound and slowly turned toward the ancient Lombardy poplar tree that must have been planted by the original homesteader. There, scarcely a dozen feet away, sat a great horned owl perched on a low limb. Dave closed his eyes, and when he opened his eyes once again the moon was passing behind a cloud. The owl had not moved. It was watching Dave with focused curiosity. The bird blinked yellow-rimmed eyes, ducked its head, blinked again. Dave cupped his hands around his mouth and blew hot air to warm his fingers. He went inside.

There were many nights when Dave could not sleep. He would get up and go about a familiar routine. He opened the stove door, fed in chunks of wood, shut the door with his foot and watched the fiery coals ignite the wood. Sometimes Peggy or one of the girls got up early and saw Dave standing outside on the deck facing Houston Lake. He would be wearing jeans and a western shirt, standing in stocking feet, unshaven, his flesh tightly gripping the bones in his face, brown eyes watchful, shoulders slumped and his head hung low. Standing out there like that gave him the appearance of an old stump.

It was times like these, at night and in the early light of morning, when Dave felt an aloneness that was like a distant howl. He stared off across the mirrored sheen of Houston Lake; saw the comings and goings of the great blue herons, the way the black ravens traipsed down the sky, and he listened to the soft lowing of the cattle, or a farmer miles away start up a piece of machinery. Sometimes he glanced off to the south, in the direction of Powell Butte, the long hill humped like a misshapen spine. He wished for another horse like Goliath; hot, eager and ready to work. With a good horse under him all it would take was a roll of his tongue or a slight nudge with spurs to ignite action. Dave mused how much simpler his life would be if he had been content to just stay put on the home ranch in Dayville, marry Peggy and raise their family there. Why had he ever been so damned ambitious? What did ambition ever buy him but heartaches? It was ambition that drove him to the devil; ambition stimulated his need for alcohol—just one to jumpstart his day—but it was never just one. Dave felt a muted cry begin down deep in the pit of his stomach. It inched its way upward and came to life as a groan. Dave's need for alcohol was that great. All he could do in response to his craving was to brush a futile hand over his head, making the hair rise and fall as high grass rises and falls in the wind.

*****

Over the intervening years since high school, Dave had maintained a casual connection with his basketball coach, Dennis Lacy. Every few years one or the other would call and talk about old times and catch up on what was happening in each other's lives. Dave recalled his years playing high school basketball with fondness and could not imagine where all the years had gone. He would like to be allowed the indulgence of going back to the locker room before a game and soaking in all the pleasant sensations; hearing the clop of the heavy work boots on the bleachers as the crowd filtered in, smelling the stale gym clothes and stiff sweat socks, to see the pink of naked feet on cold concrete, the feel of tying the white laces on black high-top Converse shoes, Coach Lacy's voice booming encouragement over the heads of eager boys, the clobbering roar when the home team took the floor for warm-ups, to feel the spinning ball touch his fingertips, driving hard to the hoop, one dribble, shoot ... those had been some of the best moments of Dave's life and he wished he could go back in time.

Coach Lacy was a big man, from Kentucky, and he had managed to maintain, at least in Dave's mind, an aura of indestructibility. Now he called Dave and they bantered back and forth. Dave asked Coach Lacy where he was living and the reply was, "Texas." Coach Lacy went on to explain that he was being treated for cancer in Dallas. Coach Lacy had always been a hard smoker—unfiltered Camels—two to three packs a day, and Dave asked if it was lung cancer.

"Yup," said Coach Lacy. "Guess the cigarettes finally got me. Haven't told a soul, but wanted you to know."

Dave asked, "Have you made your peace with God?"

"I've been doing a little bit of studying for my final exam," said Coach Lacy. "I want to make sure I don't fail. So, if you've got a moment, let's do it right now."

Dave prayed for his coach. He never asked God to cure the cancer, only that He forgive Coach for any transgressions, and that He welcome Coach Lacy into His heavenly fold.

After that, while Coach Lacy was going through radiation and chemotherapy treatments, he called Dave every other week or so. With each visit, Dave could tell Coach was getting weaker and weaker. The last conversation they had, Coach Lacy said, "Dave, if I don't have the opportunity to see you again on this earth, I'll catch up to you on the other side." Coach Lacy died two days later.

*****

The national economy was improving and Dave was finding enough work to keep busy and earn a living for his family. He had been sober for several years and firmly believed his hard drinking days were behind him; a dark mark in his sordid past, although he had never lost his desire for drink and continued to crave alcohol.

Dave was a relatively young man, and yet he was like a grizzled mountain man who reminisced about the way the county used to be when it was wild: the grasses, the game, the big skies, the mountains and valleys—the glory of it all.

Dave was of a different era. He was nostalgic for those years when building was booming and the money rolled in, but he had resigned himself to the fact those days were over and gone and never coming back.

The Franke family had been forced to downsize. The six-bedroom, six-bathroom mansion on top of the hill overlooking Houston Lake was sold. They moved into a new place at the foot of the lake that consisted of three logging camp bunkhouses that had been strung together. Dave remodeled the existing structure, and added on rooms using mortise and tenon construction that opened onto a magnificent view of Houston Lake.

Chuck Boardman, the eccentric retired attorney and former Deschutes County district attorney and municipal judge, called and invited Dave and Peggy to a get-together he and his wife, Frances, were having Friday evening at their house in Bend. Dave had built the Boardmans' lovely custom home and he felt a responsibility to attend, especially since it was Chuck who had given Dave his start in construction by turning over his Dobbin Acres subdivision. Dave promised to be there, but Peggy had plans; she was going to be busy running their daughters to birthday parties and school functions.

When Dave arrived, the party was in full swing. The guest list was an impressive array of influential associates, friends and neighbors. Everyone was drinking and having a good time. Dave had a glass of water and visited. Frances, who loved to play the piano, took her seat at the piano bench and began playing, taking sips of red wine between songs.

"Have a little wine with me," Frances begged Dave.

"Not now," said Dave.

"One little glass of wine isn't going to kill you," chided Frances. She flashed a smile, and although Dave had been sober for a long, long time, he supposed he could handle one innocent glass of red wine. Besides, wine was not like whiskey. Wine was a lightweight drink. It only took a moment for Dave to convince himself that, after all, in a social setting such as this, maybe he could handle a small glass of wine.

After having a few sips of wine Dave allowed Frances to coax him into singing. She said how much she loved his baritone voice when he had sang on previous occasions. She resumed her seat on the piano bench and set her glass of red wine aside. Her fingers quickly found the keys and she launched into a rollicking rendition of *How Great Thou Art*.

It was an ironic twist, or perhaps merely a coincidence, that Dave took childlike sips of the wine and sang a tribute to God. It was a song that the congregation at his father's church in Dayville often sang, and Dave—his voice resonating like Thor, the god from Norse mythology associated with thunder and lightning—did that song justice. As the voice, the words and the music swept over them, the revelers in the room were in absolute awe. Dave sang:

Oh Lord, my God
When I in awesome wonder
Consider all the works
Thy hands have made

I see the stars
I hear the rolling thunder
Thy power throughout
The universe displayed

Then sings my soul
My Saviour, God, to Thee
How great thou Art
How great thou Art

Then sings my soul
My Saviour, God, to Thee
How great thou Art
How great thou Art

When Christ shall come
With shouts of adulation

And take me home
What joy shall fill my heart?

Then I shall bow
In humble adoration
And there proclaim, my God
How great Thou Art

Then sings my soul
My Saviour, God, to Thee
How great thou Art
How great thou Art

Then sings my soul
My Saviour, God, to Thee
How great thou Art
How great thou Art

How great Thou Art
How great Thou Art

Dave's flourishing delivery was so powerful—and it might also have had something to do with the amount of alcohol the guests had consumed—that caused tears to be unabashedly shed by every woman and man in the room. With the power of the last note still vibrating the air, the partygoers cheered lustily and demanded a repeat performance. Before Dave could comply, his wine glass was refilled. He sipped and he sang, and later that evening, feeling in high spirits, Dave did not protest when, instead of wine, Chuck Boardman served him a tall highball filled to the brim with single malt Scotch whiskey.

The following day, as Dave went about his business of overseeing the various construction projects he had going, he stopped at the liquor store and purchased a half-gallon of Scotch. His reasoning was that he could take a little nip once in a great while, and it would help to even out the rough parts of his day. He told himself it was no big thing. He could take alcohol or leave it. He was choosing to consume alcohol in moderation. If there was a problem, he could quit cold turkey as he had done before.

Dave had forgotten about the voices, the fight for his soul that God and Satan had waged in the Mojave Desert, the terrible delirium tremens that had very nearly killed him. The demon had him once again.

*****

It took Dave better than a week to drink that first half-gallon. He was driving on Houston Lake Road, not far from home, and went to have a little nip just to wake himself up and give him energy, but all that remained in the bottle of Scotch was a couple of wayward drops. It surprised and disheartened Dave that the bottle was empty. He stopped along the road, got out of his pickup and stood, leaning against the hood in the glaring sunshine. Overhead a hawk and a raven passed going in opposite directions. Nearby a flurry of little birds, whistling cheerfully, busily worked the tumbleweeds caught in the fence wire. Dave hardly took notice. His attention was not on his surroundings, but on the taste of those few drops he had coaxed from the bottle and how much they were reminding him of his ravenous need for alcohol. He had regrets, sure he had regrets. Life did not always give a fellow a fair shake. Did he have battle scars to prove life was not fair? Hell yes he had scars. He had fought his demon in the desert, and it had damned near done him in. But Jesus thought he was worth saving. He had walked with Jesus, and when he asked Jesus if he remembered, Jesus had said, *I don't remember.*

Dave reasoned, "If Jesus can forgive me for all the shit I've pulled in my life, He sure as hell will forgive me if I grab another bottle."

*****

For Dave, resuming drinking was like falling off a familiar cliff. As he went back to his old habits, old ways, old friends, his dominant personality came to the forefront once more. He was more assertive and aggressive in his business dealings. He became the general contractor for an apartment complex in La Pine, as well as the builder of a subdivision in Redmond and another in Salem. Dave's energy level, fueled by booze, was seemingly limitless. He had his nerve back. He was in control. He was top dog. The way Dave had it figured, why the hell should he hold back, stay sober and lead a life of mediocrity? For what? So he could be mediocre twenty years on down the road? Hell, he wanted to burn up all the life he had coming and go out in a blaze of glory.

Peggy saw the familiar warning signs that Dave was drinking again, drinking on the sly. She chose to simply ignore what she knew. In reality, Peggy was powerless to stop Dave—Dave was going to do what Dave was going to do—and Peggy resolutely defined her role as that of protector of her daughters and family peacemaker. She helped to hide Dave's drinking, and she smoothed out the wrinkles that Dave left behind as he bulldozed his way back into the construction industry.

Dave once again became the happy-go-lucky drunk he had always been, except when he felt someone was trying to cross him, and then his anger flared and he was ruthless. He drank with friends and he drank alone. He rarely talked about his godly vision, but still professed his faith and insisted the family attend church every Sunday. On those weekly occasions, Dave fortified himself with alcohol, drawing his daughters in as enablers to his addiction, having them fix him what he called, *my little toddy*, a combination of orange juice and vodka. He often sent them scurrying back to the kitchen with the admonishment to put a *splash* more of the clear *toddy* mix in his drink.

"This much more," he would encourage, holding his thickset fingers a couple of inches apart; taking a gulp of the drink so there would be more room in the glass for his *toddy*.

Dave was never mean or belligerent when he drank; quite the contrary. When he drank he often became reflective, philosophical and tender to the point where he could easily make his daughters feel awkward and even uncomfortable. If it was a Saturday morning and the girls had had girlfriends spend the night, they awoke to find Dave in the kitchen, fixing bacon and French toast, with his ever-present toddy clutched in whichever hand was not holding the spatula. He often called the girls by number instead of by name, one being the oldest; down to four being the youngest. He might say, "And here is my number one girl; so pretty and full of fury and fire." To another he might say, "My little princess number three is up and ready to attack the day. I love you."

When he was being tender, Dave could easily become emotional, to the point of tears. He wore those tears like badges of honor, to show his love and commitment to his family. But that sort of sentimentality easily embarrassed the girls. In church Dave required the girls to stand beside him, and if one of his daughters was not singing loud enough, or not paying proper attention to the sermon, Dave reached over—hiding his hands under the girls' long hair—and squeezed the thin bands of muscles on either side of their necks in a vice-like grip. The girls were not allowed to show pain or any type of emotion; they just had to take the punishment their father meted out.

Chapter Eight

It was Mark Twain who said that every man is a moon with a dark side that he does not allow anyone to see. But everyone was aware of Dave Franke's dark side, and it was inevitable his constant drinking would eventually cause serious damage to his health. He had suffered from high blood pressure since he was 37 years old and had found that when he drank hard, which was most of the time, he had to take higher and higher doses of the medication to regulate his blood pressure. For more than two long decades Dave got away with playing this deadly game of pills and booze.

Then, one summer day when Dave was in his early 60s, he was flood irrigating in the pasture and suddenly he felt lightheaded, like he was going to pass out. He was holding a shovel at the time and used both hands to slide down the handle. He sat on the ditch bank and slumped over until his chin was resting on his knees. His vision became distorted and narrowed and constricted. It seemed to Dave as though he was looking down the barrel of a three-inch sprinkler pipe. He was sweating profusely; there was a peculiar tightness in his chest, and it was hard for him to draw a breath. His stomach was queasy, and to relieve some of the pressure he was feeling Dave belched loudly. That action seemed to temporarily alleviate his nausea, steady him and take away some of his pain. After a good 15 minutes or so of just sitting there, Dave regained his senses and the symptoms slowly ebbed. He sat and watched a mountain bluebird land on a juniper fencepost, and a goshawk make a tight pass over Houston Lake, flushing a flock of red-winged blackbirds which called caustically. The hawk flared off to perch on a dead limb in one of the Lombardy poplar trees. The blackbirds scattered back into the safety of the tall cattails. Dave knew that at a certain point the deadly game would resume and he watched with interest, carelessly passing off his symptoms of a heart attack as some fluky thing caused by his reaction to his blood pressure medicine.

That night, while Peggy was busy in the laundry room, Dave had another episode. He was on the way to the kitchen to refresh his *toddy* when his heart fluttered, skipped a few beats and then made up for it with a series of rapid, strong beats. Dave lost his balance and dropped to one knee. He was able to steady himself without going all the way down and remained in that position for several long moments, unable to move. Finally, knowing he could not stand, he crawled on hands and knees to his recliner and drew himself up and onto the chair. The exertion made it seem to Dave as if his heart was flipping over in his chest. He thought he was going to vomit, was short of breath and sweat popped from his forehead and face like he was a cartoon character. His nose bled, a rush of crimson ran over the grimace of his clenched lips, down his chin and neck and stained his shirt. What Dave thought was, *This is the end*, and he accepted it without reservation or feeling regret for all he would miss, or any culpability for having pushed his body to the point where it had broken.

Peggy came in from the laundry room, found Dave in this dire condition and immediately announced she was calling an ambulance. Dave stopped her. He lied and said he was feeling better, that it was just a momentary thing caused by his blood pressure medicine. Finally, he promised to visit the doctor the following day.

Dave spent the night on his leather recliner, and in the morning Peggy drove him to his doctor's appointment in Redmond. Dr. Daniel Murphy listened as Dave explained what he referred to as *my little episode*. The doctor ordered a battery of preliminary tests. At the conclusion of these tests Dr. Murphy abruptly left the room. The door remained open and Dave listened as the doctor made a hurried phone call.

"I have a young man here," Dr. Murphy said, "and I'm not at all sure if he can make it, but I am going to AirLife him over to you."

The side of the conversation that was audible to Dave, about the "young man" and his need for AirLife, made Dave think the fate of another patient was being discussed. Dave felt concern for the poor fellow that was to be flown by AirLife, and the fact that this man might not live through the ordeal. Then Dr. Murphy returned, gently patted Dave's shoulder and said, "You're going to take a little ride."

"I am?" asked Dave. "Where am I going?"

"To Bend in a helicopter."

Dave suddenly comprehended that he was the patient who was to take the AirLife flight. He was the one who might not make it. This realization caused his heart to miss several beats and then hurry to catch up. There was a flurry of activity around Dave as nurses rushed to ready him for the upcoming flight. He was transferred from the examination table to a gurney and taken outside to the landing pad where the helicopter, blades whirling, was waiting. The wind was blowing fiercely and it swept away the gown covering Dave, leaving him exposed, wearing only his shorts. He was lifted into the helicopter and strapped in place. The engine changed pitch and the pilot shouted over the noise, "The flight takes six minutes. Can you hang on six minutes?"

Dave could manage only a single word. He said, "Yup."

Before this nightmare began, Peggy had run across the street to pick up some medications from the clinic pharmacy. As she was walking back to the doctor's office she heard the rush of a helicopter launching itself into the wind and flying south toward Bend. She saw the red light on the belly of the aircraft throbbing like a severed artery and had not the slightest inkling Dave was in that helicopter. After returning to the doctor's office, and learning what had transpired, Peggy drove to St. Charles Medical Center and took refuge in the waiting room.

Doctor Young was the cardiologist who examined Dave. He made a passing comment that there was nothing he could do for Dave. One of his nurses heard that proclamation and hurried to the waiting room to tell Peggy what Dr. Young had said, that there was nothing that could be done for Dave.

But that was only a tiny sliver of what the doctor had intended. What he was actually saying was that nothing could be done for Dave without performing open heart surgery. Doctor Young informed Dave, "We have moved you to the top of the list. You are ahead of all the other surgeries. In the morning you will undergo surgery to fix your heart and save your life."

Peggy was told this news, and she immediately went to Dave's room to be with him. They talked for a while and then Dave said, "Why don't you go home, take a shower, have something to eat and get some rest. Come back bright and early in the morning."

"I want to stay with you," insisted Peggy.

"I don't know what tomorrow will bring," said Dave. "I kinda need to be alone. God and I need to have a talk."

That night, as Dave lay in that sterile hospital room, he was confronted with thoughts about his life and how he had chosen to lead that life. He asked God if there was anything he needed to straighten out before morning and God answered, not in an audible voice, but Dave became aware of the first scripture in Genesis. Not that Dave knew the verse by heart, but he remembered it was about man's mission in life was to replenish the earth. With four daughters, all married, and grandkids, Dave had certainly accomplished his life's mission. Was that it? Was that all God wanted from him? The nurse came in and gave Dave a shot. He slept.

When Dave awoke, about 4 a.m., there was a steady stream of activity as several nurses were busy prepping him for his surgery. They shaved Dave's chest and washed and scrubbed his skin with an ugly brown liquid. A few minutes before six, he was placed on a gurney and rolled from the room.

Dave was very anxious. He felt doubtful that he could face the operation unless he could see Peggy first—just see her for a moment he told one of the nurses—but there was no stopping the prearranged cycle of events as he was wheeled down a long hallway toward the operating room. The gurney came to an abrupt stop. Peggy was there, leaning close and kissing Dave on his forehead. He felt the trembling of her lips, and smelled the freshness of soap and the fragrance of her perfume. Then she was gone and his journey continued. Dave called out, "I love you," and his sudden utterance sounded sad and pathetic, like the final words of a dying man. Dave never intended that and tears sprang from the corners of both his eyes. He bit his lower lip.

The operating room was painted a happy sterile blue. It was cold in there, but action was brisk and especially confusing to Dave as he watched five nurses—three women and two men— scurry from one task to the next. Dave was placed on what to him seemed like a very narrow plank, and he was aware enough to instinctively know the padded plank would be used as a point of leverage to open up his chest when his breastbone had been severed. A face leaned close and a cavernous mouth asked if Dave had any questions.

"Just one," said Dave, and his voice was harsh and hardly more than a raspy whisper. "When you pop me open like an oyster, how are you going to put me back together?"

The face explained in clinical terms how bands would be affixed to hold the breastbone together and how, in time, the bones would fuse. Dave was instructed that for the first few months he would not be able to pick up anything weighing more than 13 pounds, or risk tearing loose the bands.

"Why don't you use heavier bands?" was Dave's response.

The face smiled and began to retreat.

"Can I still ride my horse?" asked Dave.

But the face was gone and the question went unanswered. Dave had the sensation of slipping off the narrow board, and he made a feeble attempt to move and center himself, but his conscious mind was gone as he fell under the full effects of the anesthesia.

*****

Upon awakening, Dave was aware of an obstruction in his throat. A fat tube was protruding from his mouth and Dave rolled to one side and tried to yank out the tube. A nurse caught him in the act, and when Dave fought the nurse he was quickly subdued and his wrists were strapped to the bedrails with Velcro strips. Dave was having difficulty drawing a breath. He was in a panic, could not talk with the tube down his throat so he made signs that he needed something on which he could write a message. The nurse provided a tablet and a pen, held the tablet in front of Dave's right hand and he scribbled his message on the paper. He wrote, "I am dying!"

The nurse swiftly stepped to the IV tube that was feeding medication into Dave's body. She inserted the needle of a syringe, depressed the plunger, and almost immediately Dave drifted into a deep sleep.

Dave awoke and saw the same nurse dressed in white sitting at the foot of his bed watching him. His arms remained tied to the bed frame. It was at this point that Dave thought, *This is not a good day*.

When Dave finally awoke, and the breathing tube had been removed, he was encouraged to get up and move around. At first he was unsteady on his feet and needed help to maintain his balance. When he was finally able to walk on his own he paced the hallways, breathing in the odors of antiseptic, listening to the rattle of bed rails being lifted into place, buzzers buzzing, the squeak of rubber-soled shoes on floor wax and the hush of wheelchairs being pushed down the long corridors. As he passed a room an old man might groan with his pain or someone would sigh heavily in their sleep. Other than the subtle sounds of sickness and the comings and goings of jaunty visitors, the hospital was mostly a quiet, dark, dank place; a place Dave did not want to be.

On the sixth day, as Dave was dressing to leave the hospital, he happened to glance in a mirror. The reflected image was that of a haggard man with an ugly purple scar running from the base of his neck downward nearly to his navel. The thought that came to Dave's mind was, *That was a close call. Guess You haven't given up on me yet, God*. He finished getting dressed and Peggy drove him home.

Peggy was working full-time as the assistant manager of the Crook County Fairgrounds. She did not want to leave Dave alone at the house and made arrangements to have her mother come stay with Dave during the day while he was recovering from his four-way bypass operation. But after only a few hours, Dave called Peggy at her office and said, "Honey, it's a lovely thing you're doing to have your mom babysit me, but I don't want her here."

Dave sent Ruby away, and as soon as she had departed, he went directly to the liquor cabinet, hauled out a bottle of Scotch and proceeded to drink the entire bottle. When Peggy arrived home from work and saw the empty bottle sitting beside Dave's chair she could not believe her eyes. She asked the obvious question, "Have you been drinking?"

Dave's reply was, "Leave me the hell alone."

*****

Peggy had thought, with the miracle of the heart surgery behind him, Dave would be thankful and mellow and less driven, confrontational and controlling. But to compensate for what Dave saw as his vulnerability, and his body's weakness, he turned more than ever to alcohol to sustain his energy and nerve. The combination of pain pills and other medication, mixed with booze, was a near lethal concoction that changed Dave's personality. No longer was he the happy drunk and the life of the party. Now he was moody, sullen, withdrawn and judgmental. When he talked, he often slurred his words, and there were times when he was unsteady on his feet.

This new Dave was especially critical of Peggy; nothing she could do ever pleased him. Peggy responded by trying to smooth things over, to go along, to get along with whatever Dave wanted, with whatever he said.

Peggy had always enjoyed her independence. She was the one who was responsible for running the household and raising the children. That had changed, and now she was at the mercy of Dave's unrealistic demands. He wanted to know every last detail of how she spent her days. He asked for her opinions about everything from current world events, to something related to the house, or maybe it was only to make a spiteful comment about dinner. Once Peggy expressed her opinion, Dave took the opposite side and his argumentative points were aimed at belittling Peggy.

Their marriage had deteriorated to the point where Dave and Peggy were separate islands surrounded by the turbulent waters of life. They remained so far apart neither could ever make the long jump from one island to the next. All they could do was stare at each other in the far off distance. Peggy felt her poise and self-confidence erode. She became uncertain and full of self-doubt and suspicious of Dave and his motives. To put it bluntly, Peggy lost her way. She even lost her ability to lean on the Lord in her time of greatest need. With her daughters grown, married and with families of their own, Peggy felt abandoned and alone.

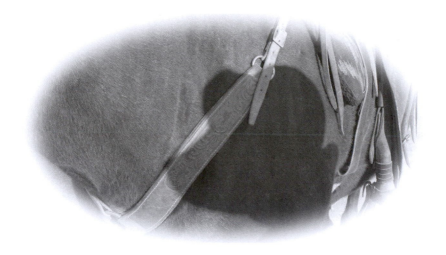

Chapter Nine

Dave had done everything he could for his father. He bought the home ranch to free his father from a mountain of debt. He bought new pickup trucks when Milo wanted a new rig to drive. Even into old age Dave was taking care of Milo, paying his bills at the apartment in Sutherlin where Milo and Evelyn were living. When Milo passed away, Dave took care of his father one last time.

At Milo's graveside service the funeral director refused to close the grave until all the expenses were paid in full. The Franke family stood together as a group, saying nothing. It was Dave who stepped forward and inquired, "How much?"

The funeral director stated the amount, "Eight hundred dollars."

Dave removed his checkbook and on his father's casket wrote a check, handed it to the funeral director and said, "Button 'er up."

As Dave and Peggy were walking away, Dave was thinking about how any obligations and responsibilities he had owed his father were now paid; paid in full. He had never found joy in taking care of his father or other members of his family when they requested money. He merely signed the checks and did not ask, or expect the money to be repaid. He could not afford to do that anymore.

Dave went back only once to view his father's grave. The headstone he had ordered was in place. Words were engraved in stone, name and dates of birth and death, and the special inscription, *A Man Who Loved The Lord*. Dave knelt on one knee and his fingers tenderly traced the cuts in the stone. Around him other stones sat at odd angles, either bowing to the prevailing winds, or yielding to the saturation of the valley rains. The ground over his father's grave was mounded. Squares of sod were beginning to weave themselves back together. Dave cried.

*****

For several years, death haunted the Franke family. In addition to the passing of his father, Dave lost his mother and oldest sister. Peggy lost both of her parents. Dave tried to hide, or at least to mask his grief with even more alcohol. He was deep in the throes of alcoholism and very seldom allowed himself to feel any joy, or happiness; only pain and self-loathing. God had been relegated to a far back burner. Dave was causing Peggy to suffer too. She no longer had the strength to fight against Dave's critical and controlling ways. She was submissive and attempted, by any means available, to reduce any threat of friction in their fragile relationship.

*****

Alcohol will eventually burn a hole in a man's stomach the way sun through a magnifying glass will burn grass on a hot day. For several weeks, Dave was besieged with stomach pains, and then the pains increased and he was not able to sleep or keep anything down, even alcohol and water came right back up. It was only when he was hit with excruciating stomach pains that he finally gave in and agreed to see a doctor. Dave did not like doctors. They were always asking if he was a drinker, and Dave's standard reply was a lie. "I'm a sociable drinker," he would say. But now the cumulative effects of booze had finally done serious damage, and after his medical examination Dave was scheduled for emergency surgery at St. Charles Medical Center in Redmond.

After the surgery—13 inches of his large intestine was removed—when a friend telephoned, Dave said, "They filleted me like a salmon. This is a tough one. I don't know if I'll survive."

While still in the recovery room, Dave began to badger the nurse for a drink, four fingers would be about right, and he said he was not particular; Scotch, bourbon, or whiskey, even a cold beer would do.

"I don't think that would be advisable," replied the nurse. "You need to take better care of yourself."

"A drink is the best way for me to take care of myself," reasoned Dave.

*****

Dave was sent home from the hospital with specific instructions that he adhere to a soft, bland diet. He ignored those instructions and raided the refrigerator, ate anything he wanted, and continued to drink alcohol deliberately, grimly, joylessly. Dave was moving headlong in the direction of his own self-destruction. Peggy felt there was nothing she could do to alter the inevitable course of events that would surely have to play themselves out, and so she simply retreated and tried to stay away from Dave. The silent house seemed to grow bigger; the hallways longer, and the distances between rooms greater. The effect was that every footfall threatened to send a violating tremor echoing through the house as Dave moved between his recliner and the kitchen where the food and booze were kept. After two days of this deliberate warfare, Dave was rushed back to the hospital for additional surgery.

Dave came through his second major stomach surgery—a blockage had shut down his small intestines—and after a lengthy stay in recovery he was transferred to a private room. The room was dark; the only light came from monitoring machines and a crepuscular glow showing from the hallway through a narrow slit where the door had been left slightly ajar. Dave glanced toward the foot of the bed, to the mirror fastened on a cabinet door, and the image he saw within the narrow confines of the frame horrified him. It was Dave's face, but he was much, much older. His sagging, wrinkled skin was like that of a 100-year-old man, not a man in his early 60s. Even more alarming was the color of his skin, a fiery red. But the determining factor for Dave was the nubs of black horns protruding from the scalp. He tried to blink away the disturbing image. It remained firmly etched in the mirror. It was Dave's face, and it was the image of Satan.

Dave brought a hand up near his face and a hand came up in the mirror; the only difference in the reflected likeness was the devil was holding a cigarette. Dave watched the tip of the cigarette glow bright orange, and sapphire smoke ooze from the devil's mouth. A stream of smoke clouded the devil's face for a brief moment and then cleared. Dave dropped his hand, and the hand of the devil dipped below the level of the mirror. Dave tried it again. The same thing happened. He looked around for the emergency button to call a nurse, but he could not locate the device.

Dave kept dozing, and each time he awakened, he was staring into the repulsive reflection in the mirror. As far as Dave knew, a nurse never came to check on him. He remained alone in the room with the devil. He blamed the crazy apparition on the drugs they were giving him. The drugs were making him hallucinate. Eventually Dave came to accept the image as real and all he could do was to acknowledge the devil and say, "Okay, you son of a bitch, you won. You finally got me."

While Dave was hospitalized, fighting his battle with Satan, Peggy was busy praying the night away, asking God to spare Dave. During this latest ordeal she had lost even more weight. Her elbows, wrists, knees and ankles stuck out on her lean body like knots in a length of rope. She was worn out, desperate, miserable and had nothing more to give beyond tears of pity. When morning finally arrived, Peggy did something that was totally out of character for her to do; she went to the well-stocked liquor cabinet in the kitchen, removed every bottle of booze from the cupboard and deliberately poured the contents down the drain.

*****

Dave was discharged from the hospital and came home feeling as though his insides had been put in a blender and then poured back into his body. His energy was gone and he hurt all over. He had to have a drink, and when he discovered the liquor cabinet was empty he was furious. The arteries on either side of his neck expanded, throbbed and he cursed loudly, demanding to know from Peggy, "Why the hell did you go and do that?"

Peggy stood her ground, told Dave, "If I had had the nerve to do that years ago, I could have saved us both a lot of misery."

Dave begged Peggy to drive to town to get a bottle; said all he needed was just enough for one big slug to ease his pain and to settle his stomach. Peggy refused. Dave pleaded, whined, cajoled. When Peggy steadfastly stuck to her guns, Dave seethed and he raged.

Finally, when Peggy had reached the limit of the verbal abuse she was willing to endure, she uttered a silent prayer, "God, please forgive me." She stood, looked Dave straight in the eye—though it looked to Dave at that moment that she looked straight through him—and announced, "I can't live like this."

Dave came to her. His six-foot four-inch frame towered over her, threatened her, but Peggy did not back away. She was questioning herself, why had she stayed married to Dave?

Was it out of a sense of loyalty or was it the same level of commitment that had kept her mother married to her father and his addiction to gambling? Peggy reached inside herself and found the strength she did not know she possessed to become shockingly honest with Dave, telling him, "I've done everything I can to make you happy. I can't do this anymore. I can't stay and watch you kill yourself; I just can't."

Before Peggy turned away, she looked up at Dave with eyes so squinty it was as if she was looking directly into the sun, and there was anguish and suffering in those eyes; there was grief and sorrow and despair, hopelessness and dejection and rejection and fear, and, of course, there was love. The knots of Peggy's jaw worked so hard and fast it seemed as if she would swallow what she was planning to say next. But the words did get out; each word bitten off and discarded as if it was pure poison.

"I am done with you."

*****

During all the ups and downs of their marriage, Peggy had never threatened to leave Dave. Now she was in their bedroom, hysterical in her grief that it had come down to this, her leaving, and she was crying and defiantly stuffing clothes into two suitcases lying open on the bed. In her mind there would be no turning back.

Dave, in his weakened condition, slowly climbed the stairs. By the time he reached the bedroom he felt lightheaded and nauseous. As he approached the bed he stumbled and had to catch himself against the footboard. He remained hunched over, gripping the footboard and staring at the open suitcases. The sight of them, and the clothes stuffed inside, saddened him greatly; what saddened him even more was the knowledge that he, and his alcoholism, had pushed the woman he loved to this treacherous brink. And when he looked at his wife and saw the hurt he had caused, and her determined tears, he could not help but cry too.

"Honey, I can't blame you," he managed to say between sobs. "You have every reason in the world to leave me. I haven't been a good husband, not for a long, long time. You are doing the right thing. You should leave me."

Dave wavered, unsure what else he could say, should say, might say. He was not capable of mounting a defense. He was to blame. But he did not want to drive his wife away either. He wanted her to stay and could not imagine a life without her. He wanted to shout that he loved her. He wanted to kiss away her salty tears. He wanted to make everything good between them, make it like it had been when they were first together. He did not know how to accomplish any of those things. He knew this would be one more failure added onto his lifetime of failures.

Like a drowning man suddenly seeing the surface and making up his mind to expend his last breath to reach that light, Dave saw everything clearly—whether Peggy chose to stay or leave was her decision—if Dave wanted to live he was the one who had to change. He sniffled a few times and said, "Before you leave, I want to make you this solemn promise—I promise I will never drink alcohol ever again—swear to God I will never drink alcohol again."

Dave wept openly, unashamedly. He was a sad and desperate man and he pleaded, "Peggy, will you please stay?"

Peggy was hesitant. She was like a skittish horse that does not know whether to bolt from its stall and run away, or back up deeper into the darkness. She was weary; weary of broken promises, weary of the struggle of living with an alcoholic, weary of a husband who was not willing, or not capable of saving himself.

Dave slowly, painfully, sank to his knees. He searched for words, the right words that would convince Peggy he was worth one last chance. He prayed aloud and his voice was raspy and jagged with brittle emotions as he confessed, "Jesus, I know I have ruined my life with my drinking. I have made life miserable for my wife and our children. Jesus, I am sorry. I ask for Your forgiveness. I promise I will fight my demon. I know I cannot give in to the temptation of drink. Lord Jesus, help me with this battle. Please, help me, please." A long moment passed. Dave held out a hand and asked, "Honey, will you pray with me?"

Peggy was still sitting on the bed; shoulders slumped, crying into the heels of her hands. She knew she was not strong enough to stand with Dave and fight his demon. She was thinking she needed to get up, finish packing and leave. She just wanted to be done, and yet she had invested so much in her marriage, everything really—it was her life, her reason for being—so, how could she leave in this moment when Dave needed her the most? She allowed herself to think that maybe this time it would all be different. Maybe this time Dave really would change and become the man she had married. Peggy slowly came to a decision, and very deliberately she slid off the bed and onto her knees. She took hold of one of Dave's big hands in both of hers. They cried together. And they prayed together.

"Alone I am weak," sniffled Dave. He placed a finger under Peggy's chin and lifted her head until he was looking into her eyes. He said, "But with you, and God to help me, I know I can make it."

The strain of a long silence stretched until Dave felt that strain tearing at him—hope began to leave him—and finally Peggy whispered, "I will help you." And the two remained on their knees, praying together.

*****

Peggy unpacked the suitcases and put them away in the closet. She was not at all sure she was making the right decision, but the decision to stay had been made and she would live with it. She said a silent prayer for Dave, asking God's help.

Downstairs, Dave was sitting on his leather recliner, intently reading his Bible, searching for a scripture that might point the way and help to somehow make this drastic change in his life an easier transition. What he was really searching for was hope. Hope that he could keep his promise, hope that Peggy would not change her mind and leave, hope he could, once and for all, rid himself of his demon. The muscles in his body were rigid, holding his tension like tight piano strings. He glanced away from the Bible toward the five stately swans slowly plying the placid surface of Houston Lake, and damned if he did not want one more drink—a final drink to celebrate his decision not to drink. That thought almost amused Dave and he nearly smiled. If he had just one more drink maybe he could pull this off. One more drink.

The following night, as Dave and Peggy lay in bed, the delirium tremens attacked Dave and he began to sweat and shake and mumble incoherently about his hallucinations. Peggy had never seen what withdrawal would do to an alcoholic's body. She was afraid. When she asked if there was anything she could do—get a cold rag for his forehead, some water to drink—Dave, his teeth clinched and chattering, head bobbing involuntarily, told her, "Just hold me. Just hold me and tell me you love me. Pray for me."

Dave drew his arms and legs up and curled into a fetal position on the bed. His body shook violently—until he thought he would break apart—his heart raced and sweat squeezed from every pore to soak the bedding. Peggy curled up against Dave's back, her arms around him, holding him tightly as she whispered, "I love you," over and over again she whispered that she loved him.

In the darkness, in the moment, with Dave and his ragged breathing, Peggy turned to her faith. She put her trust in God and prayed, and prayed, and prayed some more. She asked God to ease her husband's suffering, and she prayed that Dave would remain sober for the rest of his life. When exhaustion finally did tug Dave into erratic unconsciousness, Peggy lay awake examining the wounds and deep scars of her marriage. She asked God to heal those many wounds and scars. She thought maybe she could forgive Dave, but she doubted she could ever forget. She prayed to forget. She promised to trust God to heal her marriage and to help get them through this dangerous time. Dave awoke again, dozed, and again awoke. Each time he fell back to a troubled sleep, clutched in Peggy's arms; feeling the way she touched him lightly, soothingly. She stroked his fevered forehead with her warm fingertips, she would not let him go. She prayed.

*****

Dave awoke to a morning that broke bright and clear. The air seemed washed with a summer freshness that follows a night of rain. The sky and sparkling sun were mirrored in the flat waters of Houston Lake. The crisp air magnified the clarity of the voices of Canada honkers and trumpeter swans. Dave blinked his eyes several times. His muscles were sore from his night of uncontrollable shakes, cramps and trembling. His head throbbed. His stomach hurt. His mouth was dry as cotton. He needed a drink. With a guttural moan, Dave rolled out of bed, and slid onto his knees. He folded his hand on the mattress and he prayed. "Jesus, give me strength. Give me strength to make it through this day."

Peggy had propped her head on a pillow and was watching Dave pray. It was evident she had been crying; her tears had dried, but her eyes were still red-rimmed and glistening. She told herself this time things were going to be different. This time Dave was going to stay sober. She did not know if this was true, or if she was lying to herself.

*****

Dave, alone in the house, became aware of music. The sound was very subdued, and yet powerful and arousing and absolutely the most beautiful music he had ever heard. Voices of men, women and children sang in wondrous harmony. A full orchestra played; each instrument seemed to come alive with sound. Dave strained to listen. Wanting the sound to be louder, he went in search of the source, checking the stereo first. It was turned off. The television was also off. Dave surmised a

124

radio in one of the bedrooms must be playing. He checked, but none of the radios in the bedrooms was turned on. The most peculiar thing was that, as Dave moved from room to room, the volume of what he was listening to, the intensity of sound, never varied. It remained barely audible, and yet there was no denying that incredible music. It actually did exist.

Rarely had Dave ever taken time to stop whatever he was doing and just listen to music, but now he did. It was like every atom in his body was listening and Dave instinctively knew God was somehow involved. It was God who was sending this music directly from heaven. Certainly the music was godlike. There was no denying it was godlike. Dave questioned if this was a sign from God—were the worst of Dave's delirium tremens finally over—was God answering Dave's constant prayer? *God, give me strength.*

Dave felt elated. He was filled with the heavenly spirit, but when the music abruptly ended, he was left with only silence and he wandered aimlessly through the house hoping the music would magically return. It did not.

Late that afternoon, as Dave was stepping into the shower, he turned on the faucet, and in addition to the water, sound issued forth from the showerhead, the same astonishing music as had been playing earlier. Again Dave was filled with joy. He tried to turn off the faucet so he could hear the music better, but when the water stopped flowing, the music abruptly stopped. He fumbled with the faucet, turned on the water, and the music resumed.

Dave stood in the shower, water cascading over his skin, listening to God's music. He was lost in a swirling realm of ecstasy. The beauty of the melody was beyond comprehension; beyond anything the human mind is capable of grasping. Dave wept.

When the hot water was used up, and the shower turned cold, the music stopped. And the wondrous music never returned.

Chapter Ten

Central Oregon was cold and snowy, so Dave and Peggy decided to spend a few months in a warmer climate. They drove south with their horses in the horse trailer. Their daughter, Tawnya, her husband, Rick Taylor, and their four children lived in the town of Benson, Arizona. Dave and Peggy planned to spend time relaxing with family and to do some riding on the desert. They rented a house in Tucson, boarded the horses and drove back and forth to Benson.

One Sunday, while attending the First Baptist Church in Benson, Tawnya introduced her parents to Baxter Black, a well-known western poet and humorist, and his wife, Cindy Lou. Dave shook Baxter's hand and said, "We have a mutual friend, Gary Timmerman. He lives near us in Powell Butte, Oregon. According to Gary, back in the day, the two of you had some fun times at horse and cattle shows around California."

"Sure," said Baxter, "I remember Gary."

"Figured you would," said Dave. "From what Gary said, you two lived the high life."

A look of sadness came to Baxter's face. He squinted to either shut out some of the sunlight, or the memories that came rushing at him. He nodded his head a little, as if the truth must be borne no matter how unpalatable, and in his well-practiced drawl, said, "Well, Dave, we've all lived through some of those times, but today I'd like to think I'm a better man."

With that revealing statement hanging in the air like a pregnant storm cloud, Baxter Black took his wife by the arm and escorted her up the steps to the doors of the little white church. As they walked inside, Baxter respectfully removed his trademark black cowboy hat, and held it over his heart.

Dave looked around the parking lot to where all the cars and pickup trucks wore the same rusty tint of desert dust that even a day of rain could not wash away. A churchgoer opened a car door, releasing a flash of reflected sunlight that cut like a knife blade and Dave turned away from the glare, thinking his chance encounter with Baxter Black had been a defining moment, clearly seeing the popular entertainer, whom he had idolized for his wit and ability to entertain, was just a man; a man with the guts to say he had lived through years of drinking and wild times, had set all that aside and was working hard to become a better man.

*****

Tawnya also introduced her parents to a local rancher, Ron Graves. Dave and Ron hit it off from the get-go. Ron was a big man; at six-foot-six he was a couple inches taller than Dave. He was middle-aged, 20 years younger than Dave, had close-cropped hair, incredible blue eyes, and was handsome, lean and as sturdily built as a corner post. His home ranch was at Duncan, Arizona, and he also leased ranches in Ash Canyon and the Dragoon Mountains. Dave mentioned he had brought a couple of horses with him, and that he and Peggy were planning on doing some riding.

"Maybe you'd like to come out and work cattle," said Ron. "I'm running shorthanded and could use some help."

Dave nodded, said, "Yeah, suppose I could do that." They agreed to meet the following morning.

After Ron departed, Tawnya snapped at her father, "For crying out loud, Dad, why didn't you tell him you're a cowboy, and that you've owned several ranches and know how to work cattle?"

"A man doesn't have to say it," said Dave. "Being a cowboy is something you gotta just prove."

Even though Dave was excited about the prospects of returning to what he loved the most, cowboying, Peggy had serious reservations. She and Dave had come to the desert to spend time together, and now he would be going off to supposedly help a local rancher. What was really bothering Peggy was that most ranchers she knew were either outright heathens or Sunday only Christians. They might go to church, but come Monday morning God and godly ways were set aside. These men cussed and drank and Peggy's greatest fear was that Dave would revert to his old habits; that he would break his solemn promise to her—as he had done in the past—and start drinking once again. At that point Peggy was not looking at Ron Graves as a positive influence, and this was not a wonderful opportunity for Dave to do what he loved best. What registered in Peggy's mind was this was yet another temptation, and that Dave would have to somehow muster the strength to resist it.

*****

A wall-to-wall panorama of stars was visible, splashed across the wide expanse of blue-black Arizona sky as Dave kicked his muscles awake and went about loading his horse in the trailer. Dave's horse, King, was better than 16 hands tall, coal black, except for a blaze running from between his eyes down to his muzzle. The blaze looked like an errant swipe—a brush stroke—of white paint. Dave had raised King from a colt, had broken and trained the gelding. King could go all day and hold his wind and was well-schooled in working cattle.

As Dave began driving, the night was already losing its grip. A thin smear of light was showing color along the eastern horizon and even the apex of the sky was not as dark as it had been. Stars were winking with less intensity.

Switching from town, where people tried to install a vertical world with houses and trees, garages and businesses—although they had been modest about it with low-slung structures—and into the horizontal openness of the desert, with stunted vegetation and undulating hills cut by washes and arroyos, was a revealing concept to Dave. He had never cowboyed on the desert before, but he had to figure it could not be all that much different than Eastern Oregon, except on an even broader and grander scale. He was looking forward to the challenge with enthusiasm.

According to the weather report on the radio, monsoon-type rains were predicted for later in the day and Dave had tied his slicker on behind the saddle. Heading down the ribbon of road, towing his horse trailer, Dave could feel in the steering each time King shifted his weight. Apparently King was as anxious as Dave for the opportunity to get out in the wide open and work cattle.

When Dave arrived at the Dragoon Mountains Ranch, Ron and his children were unloading horses from their trailer. The son, Chad, was tall and the spitting image of Ron. The daughter, Ashley, was flaxen-haired, built as lean as a long-distance runner and beautiful. The family was mostly quiet as they tended to the business of getting ready to ride; curry combs rasped in long strokes over the horses' hard shoulder muscles and broad backs, blankets were set in place, saddles tossed on and cinches brought up tight.

Before mounting, the Graves family formed a circle and held hands. They invited Dave to join them. Ron took off his brown cowboy hat and flung it on the ground, brim down. He looked directly at Dave and said, "Just so you know the rules up front. On this ranch we don't take the Lord's name in vain, and there will be no drinking."

"Suits me," said Dave with a grin, and he was happy to join the circle.

Ron bowed his head and began to pray, "Jesus, we thank You for this day. We thank You for the sunshine You will send our way, and we look forward to the rain that is forecast. The grasses need every drop You can spare. We pray that You will look after us and keep us safe from harm, throughout this day. Thank you, Lord Jesus. Amen."

The boy and girl echoed the "amen" as Ron leaned over and retrieved his hat. He lifted one knee and dusted off his hat with a slap across the top of his thick chaps. He crushed the hat on his head, gripped the reins in one hand, placed his left foot in the wooden stirrup and grabbed the horn of his tooled leather working saddle. The stiff leather creaked as he swung with practiced ease up and onto the saddle. He sat a horse well.

Once everyone was mounted, they fanned out and began to ride, looking for cattle as they drifted across the desert. The sun was a brightly colored peach with bands of intense light radiating down and reflecting back off the granite boulders that comprised the Dragoon Mountains. The desert lay quiet, so quiet it was almost as if the land was between drawing breaths. Minutes passed and light bled from the eastern sky with a flutter of colors that lit the veneer of the desert in a hue of soft pastels.

King shivered from the sweat chill on his back, and Dave ducked low in the saddle as the horse went under the spiny arm of an ocotillo cactus. Dave breathed in the odor of the horse, as distinctive as burnt coffee beans, and he stroked the damp hairs on King's neck. What struck Dave at that moment was a sudden notion of *pride*. He was proud of his horse, and he was proud to be out on the open range of southeastern Arizona, riding amidst this wondrous landscape, doing exactly what he loved the most, cowboying. But he was even more proud to be sober. There had been too many mornings in his life when his head pounded and his body ached. He still wanted a drink, just to put a little more sparkle in his day, and he laughed at that—as if this glorious day needed any more sparkle—and he doubted his desire for alcohol would ever subside. At least his craving was not quite as acute as it had been a few weeks before. That was what Dave was telling himself.

It truly was a fabulous morning. A cowboy in the right frame of mind just might be tempted to hum a lively little tune, whistle a little, or break out in song to have some company to share all the wonders of life with. Dave did none of those things. He rode along listening to the creaking saddle leather and the metallic sounds of King rolling the bit in his mouth. At one point King snorted and vapor pumped from his nostrils, but the day had warmed quickly and soon the sun was beating down.

There were birds that Dave had never before seen: yellow-breasted warblers, sleek roadrunners, ladder-backed woodpeckers, green-tailed towhees, white-crowned Brewer's sparrows, hooded orioles, goldfinches and yellow-rumped Townsends. There were drab little birds that flitted about, and birds of dazzling colors that smugly sat on the tops of the tallest cactus and sang clear notes that added a brilliant luster to life. A variety of hummingbirds—iridescent colors flashing—dipped and darted here and there.

Even though this was a desert, the landscape was totally different than the Mojave. The Mojave seemed dirty and dull, devoid of color, of character, of life. The Southeastern Arizona desert was composed of white sandy soil, but it looked as if God had determined that white was just too plain and boring, and to liven it up, had added rusty red to the mix. The terrain varied from flats, plateaus, washes and arroyos, to outcroppings of boulders piled on top of each other, and those formations led back to rugged mountains that stood in a silent blue haze off in the distance. The vegetation was sparse and wicked, with thorns, barbs, spikes and sharp spines. Everything that grew seemed perfectly capable of poking, gouging or ripping flesh from any man or beast foolish enough to brush against it.

King trembled and tensed, smelled the air and nickered low in his throat. Ron's horse answered as he came into view, and for a while the two men rode side-by-side. Mostly there was desert silence, but every once in a while Ron imparted a little information about some of the characters who inhabited the desert, or some history about the Apaches' claim to this land as their home. With a motion of his head, Ron nodded in the direction of the Dragoon Mountains. They were composed of ragged peaks and draws scarred by runoff, as gray and bare as healed saddle sores on a horse's back.

The deeper canyons were timbered with pine trees and boasted unusual outcroppings of giant granite boulders piled high. Ron pointed to a particularly distinctive series of stone spires—locally known as *hoodoos*—and noted this was Council Rocks. He went on to explain that Cochise, the famous Chiricahua Apache war chief, after keeping up a running battle against the forces of the Mexicans, and later the Americans— with the urging of his only white friend, Tom Jeffords—had signed a treaty at Council Rocks. Cochise agreed to stop fighting and move onto a reservation. When the old chief died of natural causes he was buried in the Dragoon Mountains at a spot now called Cochise Stronghold. Only a few Chiricahua, and Tom Jeffords, knew the exact location of the burial site, and they took the secret to their graves.

"Still quite a few petroglyphs scattered around on the underside of boulders; if you know where to look," said Ron. "I'll show you some one of these days."

Ron went on to tell, "Everybody knows the story about the Earp brothers and Doc Holliday and the Shootout at the O.K. Corral. But not many folks are familiar with the fact the youngest brother, Morgan Earp, got killed in a shootout. The remaining brothers and the posse chased down a cattle and horse rustler, Florentino Cruz, who went by the nickname of Indian Charlie; they caught up to him at a wood camp in the Dragoons. Indian Charley was captured at gunpoint, tortured and executed without benefit of a trial. Some said Indian Charlie had nothing to do with the killing of Morgan, but at that time, the Earp brothers were pretty well running the show as far as law and order went."

They reached a windmill and a few cattle that had been standing around it saw the approaching horses and riders and ran off, leaving behind a trail of dust and their distinctive smell. The wide tail of the windmill swung a little to hold the fan into a slight puff of wind that came and went. The sucker-rod clanked and shuddered down the center of a pipe reaching into the ground and with each stroke pumped cool water from the dark depths; rhythmic gushes of warm, stale water slopped over the stained sides of the big metal stock tank, bleeding off into the sand where it disappeared.

Dave had seen a similar scene on television—*Gunsmoke,* or was it *High Chaparral?*—and he told Ron, "I listen to your stories, look around at this desert, and you know, I get the impression that around here nothing has really changed all that much in the last couple of hundred years. It's still pretty much the Wild West. I half expect to look up and see a band of Apaches sky-lined on a hill, or have the Earp brothers wearing hog irons come riding up on me."

They continued on, Dave riding along the top of a long flat while Ron dropped over the edge to look for cattle in the brush along the bottom. Time swirled into a lazy afternoon and Dave watched a puffy creamy-white cloud slip over the southern horizon and come marching to the north. Within an hour that seemingly benign and docile cloud had supplanted the entire blue sky, and a deep overcast now reflected back the hearty tones of the desert.

King stepped lightly down the trail and often raised his head and sniffed at the fresh sweet odor of the coming rain. In the far distance thunder rolled like cannon volleys. Dave felt the rain in the lumbering, thickening cloud mass, and upon reaching a flat-topped adobe hut, with walls two-feet thick and big double doors on one end, Dave took refuge, riding his horse inside. Soon he was listening to the hiss of rain. Rain delicately drummed the roof, a fanning of amplified sound. He watched the deluge through the open doors, staying perfectly dry inside, though he was forced to endure the sharp stench of packrats and other critters that called the building home. The storm grew in intensity and clouds ripped their underbellies open on the distant peaks. Lightning became visible, flashing brilliantly, illuminating in intense white light the jagged granite rocks of the Dragoon Mountains. Thunder rumbled and noise bounced around the desert. The fierce storm seemed centered over the mountains and then moved on, farther east. After raining hard for a couple hours, the rain tapered off, leaving the country bathed with a clean scent. When Ron came riding past, Dave pushed his horse outside and hailed him.

"Pretty smart," called Ron, nodding in the direction of the hut. Rain was still dripping off his cowboy hat and his slicker was wet.

"Dad didn't raise no dummy," answered Dave with a grin.

"You know what that old building was used for?" asked Ron as Dave drew near.

Dave shook his head. "A packrat condominium?"

"A monkery," said Ron. "Monks lived there, but they gave it up maybe 50 years ago and moved away. You're probably the first to step inside since they left; you and your horse that is." Both men laughed.

*****

A few days after the warm rain, the desert was awash in all the colors of the rainbow. There were nondescript plants with dull flowers and plants with gaudy blossoms; tall, spindly, spiny ocotillo cactus painted with waxy, fire engine red blossoms, yellow barrel cactus, staghorn cactus both red and yellow, and jumping cholla looking very feminine, dressed in lavender with pink lace. There were yellow desert marigolds, the orange and brilliant red of Indian paintbrush, the vivid blue of poor man's weather-glass and slender white stems of the hyssop. Bees flitted in and out of the blossoms. The air was fragrant with the heavy smells of perfume. Hummingbirds flew around and songbirds sang happy tunes. It was a grand time to be horseback on the desert, and Dave allowed his senses to absorb all the beauty being offered.

*****

Sun boomed into a cloudless sky as Dave, riding the serrated edge of a plateau, watched riders below fan out across a broad flat, beating the bush and driving out cattle. In the distance the shiny Dragoon Mountains were glinting in the sun. A half-mile away, a monstrous mule deer buck emerged from the lip of the drop-off and came loping along the trail. Dave reined in King and sat watching the approach of the four-point buck.

When Dave realized the big buck was on the same trail as he was traveling, he sidestepped King, and the horse stood quietly, tipping a hind foot and dozing for a moment. The big buck kept coming, glancing occasionally at the scene below on the flat, oblivious to all but those riders, their shouts, and the cows breaking brush which snapped like distant gunshots.

Dave gripped the reins a little tighter in anticipation that at some point the buck would draw near enough and notice him and the black horse, and when it finally did, there was likely to be an explosion of sorts and more than likely one hell of a rodeo. The startled buck would go one way, the horse and rider the other. But the drama did not play out as expected. The buck with the heavy rack—one tine reverting and drooping down—kept right on trotting along the well-worn cattle trail; his gray-blue muzzle a further indication of advanced age.

In passing, the buck acknowledged Dave and King with a slight nod of his head and magnificent rack; the way two heavyweight boxing champions might acknowledge each other out of respect if they happened to pass on a city sidewalk. The buck seemed to say, "Good morning," and kept right on going. King remained as frozen as a photograph, not even breathing, and then he relaxed with an audible sigh. Dave grinned, knowing he had just experienced one of those *perfect moments* in life, and he could not wait to get home and tell Peggy all about it.

*****

When Dave had a day off, he took Peggy for long horseback rides. He showed her the many reasons he had fallen in love with this desert, pointing out the way colors materialized out of the distances—pink fading into shades of purple, violet and lavender becoming red and yellow—and expressing his appreciation for the flora and fauna, the soft and sometimes gaudy hues of the land that seemed to match the richness of the sky, the swell of hills and the way they were cut by arroyos that opened onto flats and plateaus. He pointed out various cacti and interesting rock formations. And he shared with her some of the history that he had been told.

One time, as they were riding on the Ash Canyon Ranch, Dave led the way to an ancient corral. The rails and posts were lying on the ground, a confusion of odd angles, the wood in the final processes of decaying and returning to the soil. But with a vivid imagination an observer could envision wild and frantic mustangs milling and circling inside the enclosure like marbles swirled in a glass jar, a shaggy puzzle of colors: sorrel, bay, pinto, buckskin, black, white, smoky gray. The horses would be stamping, coughing, snorting, nuzzling, biting, squealing and shuffling their feet. Smells were of open spaces, sunny skies and star-studded nights. These were wild mustangs, not domestic horses that smelled of manufactured hay and processed grain. These horses had never been touched by human hands. Their tails and manes were matted. They were direct descendents of some of the first horses introduced to the North American continent.

Dave pushed his hat back and allowed the sun to hit him full in the face. He said, "This old corral dates back hundreds of years to the days of the Spanish Conquistadors. They tried to take this country away from the Indians, but the Apache and the Comanche fought back. It finally took the full force of the U. S. Government to subdue the Indians and force them onto reservations."

Dave showed Peggy a place where rocks had been piled to form a dam for collecting water. They found a flat spot and some scattered stones where they figured a cabin, or some sort of dwelling, could have been located. They had lunch and tried to imagine what life was like for the Spaniards at this remote desert outpost. They talked like they had talked when they were young and riding through the hills around Dayville. It was a wonderful day for them to begin to fall in love with each other all over again.

*****

Dave was used to cattle docile enough to submit to being gathered and driven. The cattle of the Arizona desert were not like that. They were wild and unpredictable, refusing to cooperate, and when confronted, they were more likely to attack a horse and rider than to run away. Dave quickly learned how to flank and maneuver around the cows, making them think it was their idea to move in a certain direction.

At gather the Graves family and Dave worked as a team. The cattle—Black Angus—were brought to a holding corral where the mothers and their babies were separated. Ron roped the calves and dragged them one by one to the branding fire. Since Dave was big and husky, he threw the calves and held them down with knees in their ribs while Chad and Ashley handled the ground work. When the smoking metal of the branding iron seared into flesh the calves stretched their necks, opened their mouths, and their gray tongues fell forward onto the dirt and they bellowed and bawled. Shots were administered for blackleg, hoof rot and bad eyes; a yellow tag was affixed to an ear. Bull calves were castrated. The details went smoothly in a cloud of dust and acrid smoke. The last step was like the workings of a precision clock, the brother and sister respectfully helping to lift Dave—dressed in heavy chaps—off the calf. Dave freed the calf and it ran off in search of its momma.

Ashley brought her young son to one of the brandings. It was a cool morning on the desert and the little tyke, blonde hair and blue eyes like the rest of the clan, was decked out in cowboy gear; from his cowboy hat to a tiny pair of cowboy boots.

"Oh no!" Ashley suddenly shouted as she scooped up her child. "He crapped his pants."

She peeled off her son's clothes; hat, boots, socks, shirt, pants and shorts. "I'll break him of doing that," she exclaimed, marching to a faucet on the outside of the corral, turning on the hose and spraying a jet of cold water on her naked son, cleaning away the evidence of the mishap.

Ron roared with laughter. He told Dave, "I did the same thing to Ashley when she was a baby, and it sure cured her of crapping her pants."

*****

Clint was a local cowboy who occasionally rode when Ron Graves needed an additional hand. Clint was built like a braided rawhide rope. His hands were dark from exposure to the sun, callused from work and he had all his fingers, a rarity for anyone who makes his living roping calves and cows and rangy bulls. He had a grip like a table vice. His face was ruddy and his eyes were dark and menacing and hinted at something disturbing from his past. As he rode, he was constantly glancing around the landscape, on the lookout for danger the way a wild animal will do.

Ron had told Dave about Clint, not as a warning, but just so he would know the volatility of the man he would be riding with. Clint had been a sniper in the Army, had killed many men, and he carried the weight of those killings as a black mark on his soul. While serving in the Middle East, Clint became separated from his unit and had spent two years living on the desert and avoiding capture, before reaching a *safe house*. He suffered from Post Traumatic Stress Disorder and there were times when he could act squirrely and hot-blooded. The analogy that best suited Clint was to say he was like a stick of old dynamite with glycerin beaded on the red paper; unpredictable and capable of going off at any moment.

The cowboys all wore guns, and Clint was no exception. The Arizona desert was used to ferrying drugs, and people, over the border from Mexico. A man riding for cattle needed protection and Clint wore a .38 on his hip, but usually kept the pistol out of sight under a vest. There was some question as to whether Clint could legally pack a weapon. He was a convicted felon, and according to the story, Clint had shot a man in a bar, just winged him, and did two years in the state penitentiary for attempted murder. He never mentioned that incident except in a passing remark to Ron who passed it on to Dave.

Early one morning—the earth still radiated heat from the day before—Dave and Clint were riding in Ash Canyon and the ringing of steel shoes on the rocky trail splashed uneasy sounds in the quiet. Clint took a pack of rolling papers and plucked a single paper free. Holding the reins loosely, hands one atop the other on the horn—like a sailor leaning with indifference on the tiller, willing to allow the current to carry his boat wherever it might decide—Clint removed a tin of Velvet tobacco from an inside vest pocket and slowly began to build a cigarette, taking his time. It was as if he did not smoke often and wanted his cigarette to be made as perfectly as possible. When he finished, he did not lick the sticky part like some men do, licking the length, but he bowed and flicked his tongue in tiny licks and rolled the cigarette tightly between his thumbs and fingers. He lit the end of the rolling paper with a wooden match, holding onto that match to make sure it was dead, and then discarding it on the ground. They moved ahead and Clint puffed a time or two on his cigarette and started talking. It was so unlike Clint to do such a thing—to talk—and the words came bouncing out of him like ripe fruit falling from an overloaded truck. Dave was astonished at the rush of words as Clint told about his experiences when the oil fields were booming up north. Clint said he had traveled to North Dakota and drove heavy equipment.

"The company paid me cash under the table, and they paid well," said Clint, taking another puff from his cigarette, exhaling. "When I saved up 12 grand I up and quit, bought a new horse trailer and come home."

Since the ice between them had been broken, Dave talked a little about the time he had spent on the Mojave, about his vision of walking with Jesus, and how he had accepted Jesus into his life. He talked about his ongoing fight with his demon and how alcohol had very nearly ruined his life. Clint drew his horse to a stop. He ground out his cigarette on the leg of his heavy chaps and turned to Dave and said, "I've killed too many men for God to ever forgive me."

"You killed out of patriotism and loyalty to your country," said Dave.

Clint shrugged his shoulders. He said, "I don't know if that makes it right or not."

"All you have to do is ask for God's forgiveness," offered Dave.

Clint tilted back his hat a little, so the red of the sun hit him full in the face and said, "In that case, will you pray for me?"

Two cowboys, holding hands, sat on their horses on the windswept desert, heads bowed, and Dave prayed, "Jesus, I ask you to recognize Clint and see the many burdens he carries with him every minute of every day. I ask You to raise the weight of these burdens. I ask You to grant him forgiveness and to heal his spirit. I ask this in the name of Jesus. Amen."

After that prayer, the men once again rode in silence. At the end of the day a brilliant blush of a lively twilight fluttered across the western sky. Dave was thinking how each person has to come to grips with his or her demons. Clint had his demons; Dave had his. Dave decided the true measure of a person is in coming to grips and overcoming those personal demons that are inside each of us.

*****

Ron was the type of man who found it difficult to ever hand out a rock solid compliment. The closest he came to praising Dave and his ability to cowboy, occurred one evening as they were loading cows and horses into the stock trailer. The trailer was packed full, but Dave told King to load, and even though there was hardly room for a pony and certainly not room for an animal the size of King, the big black horse managed to wiggle his way into the trailer. Dave shut the gate and flipped the latch.

Ron shook his head and remarked, "Guess now I've seen it all. Does that horse ever make a mistake?"

"He shouldn't," responded Dave. "I broke him and trained him to never make a mistake."

*****

With the passing of each day of his sobriety, Dave could see the flicker of admiration grow in Peggy's eyes, yet he also sensed his wife was not totally convinced and feared he might backslide once again by mistakenly believing he could have a social drink or two and walk away. But Dave knew he could not have a social drink and walk away, and he accepted that as fact. Only through abstinence could Dave conquer his demon. He remained firm in his vow to never taste alcohol again.

Dave had always been decisive and able to focus on whatever task it was he wished to accomplish. He now turned his unwavering attention to winning back Peggy's love. He planned a *special date* that began one Saturday morning before daylight. He loaded their horses, King and Dundee, in the horse trailer and instructed Peggy to wear her riding clothes, suggesting she might also throw in a nice dress because he was taking her out on the town that evening. That was all he would tell her.

They trailered the horses to the Coronado National Forest at the foot of the Santa Rita Mountains, a remote section of the southeastern Arizona desert dotted with abandoned mining claims and boom towns that went bust. These had now been christened as official ghost towns. The trailhead sign pointed toward the ghost town of Kentucky Camp. The horses moved along the trail, passing through pockets of scrub oaks, mesquite and cactus. Peggy, always interested in history, asked Dave if he knew the cause of the demise of Kentucky Camp, why had it become a ghost town.

Dave was in the great outdoors, doing those things he enjoyed the most; riding horseback and spending time with his childhood sweetheart/wife. He smiled and casually mentioned there were lots of reasons why the inhabitants of a mining boom town might pack up and leave. The main reason, of course, was the mineral deposit had played out. But he said there were other reasons too; disease could rip through a town and force people to flee. There might have been a flood, or a fire, or an Indian attack.

As the horses climbed the narrow trail, Dave slowly related the history of Kentucky Camp. His words were punctuated by the sounds of horse shoes clicking and clanking against rock. As they rode, Dave and Peggy breathed in the deliciously pleasant perfumes of the desert and mountains. The unrelenting sun beat down on them. They were alone and loving the freedom and yet relishing the togetherness.

Dave said, "At one time, Kentucky Camp seemingly had it all: healthy miners, clean water, a nearby railroad and plenty of gold-bearing ore."

"So, why did it fail?" asked Peggy.

To pique Peggy's interest, Dave explained that Kentucky Camp failed because of a strange twist of fate, and the suspicious and untimely death of one man. He said the diggings were first filed on back in the 1870s when one of the largest, and richest, placer gold deposits of all time was discovered in the Santa Rita Mountains. Miners rushed in and Kentucky Camp was born as miners set up a tent town and went about trying to separate the gold from the sand and gravel. Placer mining requires water to separate the gold, but since this was a desert, water had to be hauled by burro pack trains from miles away. It took time and a great deal of effort to wash out the gold. By the turn of the century most of the miners had given up and moved away.

"In 1902 James Stetson, a mining engineer from California, arrived at Kentucky Camp and started buying up mining claims," stated Dave. "Stetson had a brilliant idea of how he could solve the water problem. He announced he would channel the seasonal runoff from the Santa Rita streams and store the water in a reservoir. Stetson believed this would allow him to tap the untold riches of Kentucky Camp. He took in a partner, a wealthy investor, who had made a fortune mining gold in the Tombstone district. The two men formed the Santa Rita Water and Mining Company."

Upon reaching a high point on the trail, Dave reined in and he and Peggy looked out over the broad vista. Behind them were the rocky and rugged Santa Rita Mountains, off to the south was Mexico and to the west and north the desert seemingly stretched to infinity. Below, in a V-shaped canyon, could be seen a small cluster of adobe buildings. Dave motioned in that direction and announced, "Kentucky Camp."

Dave finished his story by saying the principles in the mining venture were scheduled to meet in Tucson on May 21, 1905. Stetson never made it to that all-important meeting. He checked into the Santa Rita Hotel and went directly to his room. A few minutes later, a maid was startled as a body struck the window sill of the room she was cleaning, and when she looked, she saw the body of a man lying in the street. It was never known whether Stetson, a young man of only 37, might have opened a window for fresh air and fell, or whether foul play was involved and he had been pushed to his death. A formal inquest was held. The verdict was that the death had been caused by an accidental fall and Stetson's body was shipped to Oakland, California, for burial.

After Stetson's demise, the financial backer pulled out and Kentucky Camp was abandoned, until it was reborn for a time as a cattle ranch, ultimately being taken over by the United States Forest Service and a volunteer group dedicated to preserving the site.

Knowing all this history made for an interesting few hours as Dave and Peggy explored the five adobe buildings that comprised the settlement: the office of the Santa Rita Water and Mining Company, the headquarters building used to process gold samples, a small house where it was said James Stetson had lived, and the ruins of another house and a small barn, as well as the remains of an intricate water system that ran from the mountain reservoir down to the camp. By afternoon Dave and Peggy had seen everything and were headed back to the trailhead.

Upon reaching the horse trailer and pickup, Dave slipped on a clean shirt and Peggy changed into her dress. The *special date* continued as Dave drove to the town of Sonoita where he had made dinner reservations at the Steak Out Restaurant and Saloon, a chophouse famous for mesquite grilled steaks and lively entertainment. A country western band was playing, and after enjoying perfectly cooked steaks, Dave requested the band play *The Wayward Wind*. He stood, took Peggy's hand, and said, "Dance with me, darling."

Dave ushered his wife to the dance floor where he took Peggy in his arms, casually rested his right hand lightly in the pleasant curve in the small of Peggy's back. They danced, and when the romantic ballad ended, Dave bent and kissed Peggy with the same passion and intensity she had felt the first time they had kissed on that star-studded night so long ago. All the years, all the troubles and the drinking and the desperate times they had endured, seemed to melt away like ice under the heat of a blow torch. Peggy stood on her tiptoes and whispered in Dave's ear, "I love you." The band launched into the song *Desperado* and they kept dancing.

*****

Dave and Peggy had stayed in Arizona longer than they planned, but now, having said their goodbyes to family and friends, they were ready to leave. Their vacation had been fruitful; a time of healing and a time to rekindle their love. Dave had kept his promise, had refrained from drinking alcohol—not that he did not still crave alcohol, he did—but he just knew he could not afford to go back on his word and run the real risk of losing Peggy. With renewed hope for their future, Dave and Peggy were ready to head north to their home in Oregon. They planned to use the foundation they had built in Arizona to rebuild their life, a life they would share together with God.

As Dave and Peggy were walking out the door, the Graves family came roaring up, horse trailer attached to their pickup truck. Ron crawled out from behind the wheel. He walked to Dave and they shook hands. Dave might have thanked Ron and said what a golden opportunity and cathartic experience it had been for him to live his dream and be a desert cowboy. He might have said the hot sun and dry air had done wonders to dry him out and dissipate his desire for alcohol. He might have said the desert had helped him rediscover his personal pride, renew his faith in God, and strengthen his love for his wife. And Ron might have expressed his opinion that Dave had been a godsend; that before Dave came on board he had been running shorthanded and was in desperate need of a right-hand man; Dave had filled the bill. But even though both men were thinking those thoughts, neither man said any of them.

Dave gave a nod and managed to say. "Gonna miss this ol' desert. Guess I sorta got attached to it."

"You got a job any time you want it," drawled Ron.

Chad and Ashley were standing behind their father. Peggy was beside Dave, smiling. She recognized all that the Arizona desert had given Dave and her; Peggy now had her husband back, and with the Lord's help, their relationship and marriage would be restored. She was absolutely sure they were on the right path. From this point forward, there would be no turning back.

Ron removed his brown cowboy hat and carelessly flung it onto the pavement. He said, "Let's pray."

The group formed a circle, holding hands, bowing their heads. The horses shuffled their feet in the horse trailer. Ron prayed, "Lord, we are grateful to You for bringing Dave and Peggy into our circle of friends. We thank You for the many blessings You have bestowed on us. We ask that You watch over Dave and Peggy and keep them safe as they journey home to Oregon, in Christ's name, amen."

The End

New Beginnings

My Clyde,

The words I write here cannot begin to express how thankful I am that you have allowed the man I fell in love with—the man I married, and the father of our four beautiful daughters—to come back to me; only this version of you is an even better man than ever before. And now, walking hand-in-hand with my newly restored partner, I can honestly say I anxiously look forward to whatever this coming chapter of our life brings to us. We are, as always, together against the world....

I love you more than ever
Your Bonnie

Epilogue

As I look back over my life, it seems as though the constant thread has always been God. For years I thought God was my problem. I turned away from Him and chose alcohol to be my partner, my master. I alone am to blame for that.

In my early years I was obsessed with wheeling and dealing, putting business deals together and becoming financially successful. I learned to play the hand of making money and played it well, very well. I made millions. But I learned a hard and very real lesson during the years of the Great Recession in the early 1980s. The lesson I learned was that no matter how well you play the game, the federal government controls the game and manipulates the rise and fall of the economy. It is the government that holds all the wild cards, and they play them when it is to their best advantage.

R.L. Coats, my first construction boss and my mentor in business, had warned me, "Another recession is always headed our way." I didn't heed his advice and fell victim to the largest economic downfall since the Great Depression of the 1930s. I watched all I had worked so hard to achieve, my many successes, fall like dominos. Before that, I had always been the one in control of any situation, whether it was trading horses like I did when I was young, playing poker in a bar, or negotiating for a subdivision with a banker. Come hell or high water, I was the one who could make a deal work. That is the way I saw myself, a wheeler-dealer who made it happen.

I was so good at making deals I thought I could even make a deal with God. I don't know how many times, when I was drinking, I made God the promise, if He would keep me alive through the night I would stop drinking in the morning. Of course, I never kept my part of the bargain. I kept turning to that bottle of booze, and as that first drink slid down my throat I'd think this is the nectar of the Gods. And then I would turn around and drown my guilt with even more booze.

God spoke to me, said he'd have me at forty, and that was followed with, "I hope I don't have to take one of your children." I did not know if God or Satan was speaking. I was terrified and eventually learned you can't make a deal with God. But it took a lot of pain and suffering on my part and those around me who I love before that lesson began to sink into my thick skull. The only deal God is interested in making results in each of us accepting Him into our lives.

After I finally quit drinking and dried out on the Arizona desert, the hardest thing for me to understand and accept was how to forgive myself and become a real Christian, not just a religious person one day a week on Sunday. I walked with Jesus on the 101 Flat, and He said He didn't remember my sins. That was well and good, but I was not able to forgive myself. With God's help and strength I was able to starve my craving for alcohol and begin to learn the fundamentals that allowed me to forgive myself. Have I sinned? Yes, I am a sinner. Do I still have temptations? Absolutely I do. But I have learned to rely on God to get me through those moments of temptation and desperation.

This is not just a simple story about Peggy and me and our life together. This is a universal story that is bigger than the two of us. It is my hope that readers will find encouragement in our struggles, and will find the path to love, redemption and finally to restoration much more quickly than I did. And I pray these words will help each of you to become a better man/woman." *(Dave Franke)*

Life is a journey with mountaintops and lovely vistas and deep dark valleys too. Many times I have doubted I possessed the strength to withstand the depths and darkness of those valleys and yet it is those times of trouble that have made me stronger, more resilient, and better able and willing to accept God's love.

Having remained married to Dave all these years has been a difficult task. It seemed as though Dave had two very distinct personalities. I always thought of it as two opposing wolves inhabiting his body. One wolf was bad, full of anger, resentment, rebellion and guilt. The good wolf was full of love, kindness, generosity, truth, compassion and faith. I fell in love with the Dave who exhibited more of the good wolf traits, but in time the bad wolf came to dominate our life together. An old Cherokee parable tells that if you have two wolves, it is always the wolf you feed that will win. For a long time Dave fed the bad wolf a steady diet of alcohol, and that wolf thrived.

In the early years of our marriage, I was very passionate and loved Dave fiercely. We were a team, and we walked together every step of the way, achieving amazing successes. Dave was ambitious to a fault, and I was supportive to a fault. We were firm believers in the American dream—the harder you work the more you will attain—but it didn't turn out that way. I had never even heard the term "recession." But I came to learn it meant devastation and destruction. Going through the "recession" of the 1980s was like having a rug of comfort and security suddenly yanked out from under us.

I felt Dave and I were truly partners in marriage and in business, until I became the mother of our four daughters. At that point life changed. Dave began to work more and more, usually away from home, and we grew apart. While I was consumed with raising our family, Dave worked and he drank. His drinking was not something I could talk to him about. He dismissed my fears and tears with a placid smile, telling me he could stop drinking if he wanted to, he just didn't want to. I dealt with his alcoholism with an equal amount of my denial, working to cover over his imperfection and trying to keep everyone in the family happy.

During those years, my courage and confidence eroded, and rather than communicate my feelings to Dave, I simply built a protective wall around myself; nothing got inside that barrier, and nothing got out. The best way to say it is I went into survival mode. I worked very hard to shelter my daughters, to try to give them a safe and happy home, supporting them and lavishing all my attention on them. On top of that, I had business to deal with. Creditors were hounding us. I did the best I could. My intentions were good, but looking back on that time I believe I simply reacted to my circumstances and never put my trust where it belonged, in God's hands. I was just too busy trying to "fix" everything and I lost my way.

For many years I simply buried unpleasant memories in the deepest part of my heart. Revealing my emotions for this book has been extremely difficult. I have had to face issues I kept repressed for a very long time. My prayer is that our story can encourage others. With God's help you can free yourself from any predicament you are currently facing.

This story is our personal journey to find God, and to find love and forgiveness. I have had to accept the forgiveness that God provides. I have had to forgive myself and forgive Dave too. I can say with confidence and thankfulness, through all we have endured on this journey of life, that Dave has found the strength, with God's help, to become, *A Better Man.* *(Peggy Franke)*

*****

Love

Many times I look back and question, why did I waste the most important years of my life not loving my wife? We began our life together with unbridled passion. Peggy was the prettiest girl in school. When we went places, she always stood out in a crowd like a brilliant diamond. I still feel that way about her.

For many years I robbed from my marriage and allowed booze and business to rule my life. I inflicted pain on those I loved the most. I was too focused and self-absorbed, too ambitious and driven to even notice. Today I know I did not accept the responsibility of how God ordained the order of a family should be. I was not the spiritual leader of my household.

I always loved my wife, but I mistreated that love and almost destroyed it. I tried to drown my sorrow and anger and guilt with alcohol, and I watched the love in my wife's eyes growing dimmer and dimmer. My heart was breaking for what I was doing to her, myself and others, and yet I allowed my addiction to continue to destroy the love and respect of others.

One of the things I cherish most about Peggy is her ability to make any place a home, and it doesn't matter if that home is in a tent, camp trailer, or a mansion. I never appreciated that fact until I lived alone in a camp trailer on the Mojave Desert, bunked on a couch and slept in a 30-year-old sleeping bag. It was hell.

Peggy forced me to make a decision. I could keep drinking myself to death or I could have her, but I couldn't have both. I gave up booze as my mistress, and now I think and act differently. I have changed my ways. God has given me wisdom and I listen to His voice like I never did before. The love in my wife's eyes has been rekindled and today burns brighter than ever because she can once again respect me as a man. I have earned back her respect and love. I see God's hand at work on a daily basis. I pray with Peggy each morning before we leave the house. I pray a blessing over our children, grandchildren and great grandchildren. I thank God for each and know I am a blessed man. I plan to leave behind the greatest gift of all; a legacy of love. *(Dave Franke)*

Reflecting on the many kinds of love you experience in a lifetime, I believe love has many different faces, but there is one essential ingredient in long lasting love in any relationship and that is unconditional love. Only unconditional love can stand the test of time. In marriage, love is challenged by loss, by illness, by lack of attention to the relationship and the wear and tear that occurs during the storms of life.

I was married at 18 years old, so very young, but actually Dave and I probably had more going for us than most marriages do. We were raised in the same community, attended the same country school and shared common interests. We enjoyed the same lifestyle and our shared goal was to continue that country lifestyle with our children. But with time, the love Dave and I shared, changed from unbridled passion to constantly adjusting to the changes brought on by living life and raising children. We built the largest construction business in Oregon. Dave became obsessed. He was a workaholic and then an alcoholic. Somewhere along the way we failed to nurture and protect our love. The glue that held our marriage together began to dissolve.

Dave stopped drinking, but he was still controlling and meaner than a junkyard dog. He no longer had alcohol to depend on, to kill the pain of disappointments and hardships. One day in my despair I cried out to God and told God, "I don't know if I can do this anymore; it is too hard. I need a break. When is this going to get better?"

God just spoke to my heart; that nothing would change until Dave learned to love me like Christ loves His bride, the church. I didn't tell Dave about this, I kept this word from God hidden in my heart, but it totally gave me peace, and little by little I began to see changes happening. Dave became more loving, kind, considerate, and affectionate toward me. In turn, I began to trust Dave and my love and respect for him was restored.

Now when I look at Dave I see the man I first married, and not the man he became when alcohol was Dave's mistress. Our love has become deeper because it has been made stronger by the storms it has endured. I am thankful that Dave makes me feel secure and cherished, and that speaks to me of unconditional, enduring love. *(Peggy Franke)*

*****

Forgiveness

Forgiveness is an essential part of living and overcoming life. It is also the most difficult to understand and accept. I have held many things in my hands, and have lost them all; but whatever I have placed in God's hands, I still possess.

Forgiving myself is an ongoing process. I have learned I can't focus on my failures, I have to focus on what Jesus spoke to me; He doesn't remember, and I have to move forward and do the same for myself and others, or I am not practicing what I believe.

Forgiving others is not an easy concept for me. I don't necessarily forget or trust others that have done me wrong. But what I have learned to do is to consider the fact and realize other individuals need the same forgiveness that I am receiving from God who gives it to me as a gift. I can't expect to have God forgive me if I can't do the same for somebody else.

I have learned that 70 years flies by pretty quickly. My desire is to spend the time I have remaining on this earth doing things God's way, not my way. That means not dwelling on the wrongs I have done, and the wrongs that have been done to me, but to spend my time walking with God and seeing others the way God sees them.

The best part of forgiveness is that it is a healing process. Forgiveness has allowed me to become stronger and more confident. I have grown to understand that earth is not my final home, I am just passing through. My home for eternity will be my home in heaven. *(Dave Franke)*

Forgiveness and unconditional love are gifts, trust is earned. Even when I am disappointed or hurt by others, I am reminded that I am freely gifted with forgiveness and unconditional love by God. In turn, if I can forgive, then I am liberated. The most difficult thing for me to learn has been to forgive myself. Not an easy task, but if I don't forgive myself, I can't forgive others or be accepting of God's forgiveness.

In living life there have been many times when I have been hurt by Dave or others and the pain they caused me was undeserved. My choices were to hang onto my agony and wallow in my pity, or to swallow my pride, buck up, and forgive that person even when they did not deserve my forgiveness. When I have made the decision to forgive someone, I also consciously try to forget and not to dwell on the incident. Eventually the memory of the hurt that was inflicted on me will dim, and this allows me to heal. Holding on to a grudge is like drinking poison and expecting the other person to die. I no longer wake up in the middle of the night rehearsing my pain. I am continually amazed at how that godly principal works—*forgive and you receive even more than you gave.*

I have learned that if I forgive immediately and totally, and am willing to be reconciled, no situation is impossible to resolve and restore. Through the ups and downs and changes that come through many years of marriage, the only way I believe a marriage can survive is to love often and forgive often.

When Dave stopped drinking, it was not instant change for either of us. We made baby steps each day toward repairing our broken relationship. I had to learn to trust him again, and forgive him even when I didn't want to. And I had to forgive myself, for giving up on us, and desiring to just run away from him and our troubles. We made a lot of changes and learned how to forgive more, and then it made it easier to love again. Is our marriage perfect? I don't believe there is a perfect marriage, but Dave and I have accepted forgiveness and that has given us strength and brings deeper love into our marriage.

I am determined to leave the past behind and to accept the grace and forgiveness that God provides. I am thankful for each new day that is dawning. *(Peggy Franke)*

*****

Redemption

I often ponder redemption and have come to appreciate that redemption is a free gift from God. All our lives we have been taught nothing is free, that there is a price to pay for everything, but then along comes redemption. If we trust in God, if we live in harmony with God, then we will be granted eternal life. That is what redemption is all about. *(Dave Franke)*

I believe everyone is in need of redemption, not just certain people, for certain sins. Redemption is being rescued and delivered from our sin. Redemption comes through forgiveness. To be redeemed then is to be forgiven, and adopted into the family of God. With redemption comes a ransom of sorts, a ransom that was paid in full when Jesus died on the cross. The concept of redemption is probably the hardest for a Christian to accept because it requires faith in God's gift of grace. I have told God many times in my prayers, if He would just help me, I would do anything, walk on glass, go somewhere, do something, just anything that would give me peace in my heart and mind. God does not work that way, I just have to tell Him I need help and trust Him and be patient. This is not easy, but it is God's plan, and it always works if I am obedient to His ways and not mine. Redemption provides me security for the future. I know where I am going when I leave this earth. *(Peggy Franke)*

*****

Salvation

Salvation means I have been rescued, rescued from my past, and given hope for the future. Salvation is a gift for eternity. The moment I stepped into God's presence on the 101 Flat, I found the love I had searched for all my life. Time on this earth has a beginning and end for each of us. But God's love is enduring and will never end. All we have to do is accept that love and seek salvation. *(Dave Franke)*

Deliverance from the power of sin and protection from harm and destruction can only come through salvation. Only God can remove sin and deliver us from the penalty of sin. I believe we are saved through faith and repentance and believing Jesus died on the cross to pay the price for our salvation. There is only one way to receive salvation, and that is by accepting Jesus Christ as our savior. *(Peggy Franke)*

*****

Heaven

I have spent a lifetime pondering the concept of Heaven. When I had my supernatural encounters with God, I believe I caught a glimpse of what Heaven might be like. To me, Heaven is a sanctuary of perfect and eternal love. When I reach my final destination, I will ask God for just one more favor. I will ask Him if He will allow me to take care of His beautiful white horse. He is God, and I know he must have a beautiful white horse. *(Dave Franke)*

I believe this world is not my final home. I am just passing through here. Heaven is all that I have ever longed for, and will be everything I have ever needed or desired. The perfect peace and love of God will be found in Heaven. Attaining Heaven will be worth any trials or tribulations I might have faced and endured here on this earth. *(Peggy Franke)*

"A Better Man"

Dedicated to Dave & Peggy Franke
By: Tessa Lea Bailey

Wading through the pages of the story of his life. . . . The flood gates holding back the tears opened wide . . . as the words on the papers exposed his heart and pride. . . .

Reminiscing . . . *I will have you at 40* . . . those words made his heart race . . . the constant reminder of a choice he had to face. . . .

The raging storm inside his soul . . . the surrender . . . the battle to give God control . . . the desire for the broken pieces to be collected and made whole. . . .

The tug of war between good and evil . . . the conflicts he faced all his life . . . the sustaining hope in the prayers and resilience of a good and faithful wife.

His perpetual battle of guilt, hurt and shame . . . that weakened his resolve and devalued his name. . . .

The self-loathing that devoured his dreams and left wounds of pride . . . and those words . . . *I will have you at 40* . . . he ran from . . . always wanting to hide.

The alcohol that consumed him and recurrently knocks on his door . . . is no match for God's grace . . . often found in a cry for redemption on a hard and chilling floor. . . .

On knees in prayer . . . a cry out . . . a plea . . . conceding we are not the person God intended us to be. . . .

A daily walk . . . a choice . . . a stand . . . the peace that comes in finding a relationship with God . . . beholding . . . "A Better Man".

Rick Steber, the author of more than thirty books and sales of more than a million copies, has received national acclaim for his writing. His numerous awards include the Western Writers of America Spur Award for Best Western Novel, Independent Publishers Award—Best Regional Fiction, Western Heritage Award, Benjamin Franklin Award, Mid-America Publishers Award, Oregon Library Association Award and Oregon Literary Arts Award. Two of his books have been optioned to movie production companies.

In addition to his writing, Rick is an engaging Western personality and has the unique ability to make his characters come alive as he tells a story. He has spoken at national and international conferences and visits schools where he talks to students about the importance of education, developing reading and writing skills, and impressing upon them the value of saving our history for future generations.

Rick has two sons, Seneca and Dusty, and lives near Prineville, Oregon. He writes in a cabin in the timbered foothills of the Ochoco Mountains.